The
Good Girl's Guide to
Money Making

Transform Your Relationship with Money to Create More Sales in Your Purpose-Led Business

Rebecca Barr

The

Good Girl's Guide to
Money Making

Copyright © Rebecca Barr 2023
First Published November 2023
Updated March 2024
Publisher: The Femalepreneur Coach Ltd
ISBN: 9798856108643

www.thefemalepreneurcoach.co.uk

Dedication

I dedicate this book to my babies, Amelie, Brooke, Rhyley, Luciano, and Aviana, who are my greatest manifestations.

Thank you for choosing me to be your Mumma x

CONTENTS

INTRODUCTION

If my relationship with money was a Facebooks status, it would be - 'it's complicated'.

Growing up, I experienced both ends of the financial spectrum. At one end, I was made homeless twice before the age of 13; Once when my Dad passed suddenly in a car accident when I was 4, and my Mum and Sister and I were asked to leave our naval quarters, and again in my early teens when our home was repossessed. My Mum had struggled to keep up the mortgage repayments as a single parent at the time, after my Step-Dad had left us with crippling debts.

I also experienced extreme highs however after my Dad's passing too. We inherited a sum of money that saw us living the 'good life' for a while. One where we went on a holiday abroad (kind of unheard of at the time, and definitely an extravagance not seen by many in the late 80s), ate branded food and not the supermarket own label, and living in a series of houses in nice neighbourhoods. One of those neighbourhoods where everyone seemed friendly, and going to the park for hours a day, without any supervision, as long as you were with an older sibling or the other kids that lived on the street, seemed like a perfectly good way to parent your kids.

Even after our home was taken for the second time, and my Mum had become overwhelmed by spiralling debts preferring to bury her head in the sand, waiting for a solution to present itself, I continued to experience the same financial duality.

In an experience similar to Robert Kiyosaki, in his world-renowned book 'Rich Dad, Poor Dad', where his financial education came from two mentors with very opposing views, I was sent to live with family members who also held the same conflicting realities and opinions about money.

One side were considered to be 'wealthy', (although I wonder now as an adult whether they were actually 'rich' or just 'comfortable'), and the other side were not necessarily financially abundant, but were rich in other ways such as love and community.

The polarity of how each side of the family behaved and spoke about money, kicked off my life-long curiosity and obsession with it. I was fascinated when witnessing how different people acted around money; How they spoke about it, what they believed was available to them, and how their beliefs were then being reflected back to them, in their reality. The ones that spoke negatively about money, always seeming to be chasing the next paycheck. They believed that the government was out to get them, and that there was never enough, they always seemed to be struggling to make ends meet and hoping for a lottery win. The ones that were completely neutral to money however, and simply used it as a resource to live their lives, travelled twice a year, and ate, shopped and invested in what they wanted. They inevitably always had a steady flow of predictable income, that they could rely on, and build upon. Their beliefs became their own self-fulfilling prophesies. I was getting a first-hand lesson in Manifestation, before 'The Secret' was even a thing, and I was hooked.

Fast forward 10 years, and my childhood rollercoaster with money had repeated itself in my own life as an adult.

I had amassed a 7-figure property portfolio by the age of 25, after securing my first mortgage at 18, only to then walk away from 90% of it in an act of self-sabotage. I had started my venture with a partner at the time, and when my relationship broke down, rather than demanding an equitable share of the assets, I walked away with just enough for a small deposit on my next home. This was driven from a fear of being seen as money-grabbing or a bad person, as it was my decision to leave the relationship. I wanted to compensate him for this grief, even though my decision was in response to *his* actions, and he hadn't treated me as well as he should have. What blows my mind on reflection however, is that not one family member or friend advised me to act differently. Everyone agreed, that as he was super sad, I should just take what I needed and let him have the rest. Fortunately, I don't need to label this decision as a 'regret' because I know there is always more abundance working its way to me, and that, the portfolio we built, wasn't my 'one shot' at 7 figures.

After this minor setback, I slowly rebuilt my fortune, and perceived safety, within a career in corporate, only to lose it all again unexpectedly. My Mum had become my main source of childcare for my 3 young children at the time (I now have 5 – yes, I know!), and I thought I had my life set. I was a single parent but felt finally like I was starting to come into my own financially, without the support of a partner or anyone else, who could take it away from me. I had a good job, my own car, overpaid my mortgage, had savings and investment accounts for myself and my children. I thought that I had it all figured out…

It's at this point that I want to share a quote by the OG herself, Oprah Winfrey, who perfectly describes what happened next.

"Life whispers to you all the time. It whispers, and if you don't get the whisper, the whisper gets louder. If you don't get the whisper when it gets

louder, I call it like a little pebble — a little thump — upside the head.. The pebble or the thump upside the head usually means it's gone into a problem. If you don't pay attention to the problem, the pebble then becomes like a brick. The brick upside your head is a crisis, and If you don't pay attention to the brick upside your head, the crisis turns into a disaster and the whole house — brick wall — comes falling down." — Oprah Winfrey

On some level, I had always known that a corporate career in HR was not my soul's purpose in life. I didn't have the vocabulary to articulate this though, I could only describe it as an ache, every time I thought of rinse and repeating my weekly schedule for the next 30 years until I retired. I had tried to set up an Ebay business, whilst on maternity leave previously, but without the knowledge needed to give it, it's best chance of success, I barely made a sale, and had no choice but to retreat back to my predictable corporate job. I cried most days on the way to work at the thought of being away from my kids, and knowing that there had to be more to life.

That was, until one morning, when I tottered up the garden path of the bungalow I rented for my Mum, opposite my own house, in my six-inch heels. I had my son's car-seat balancing in the crook of my arm. I was rushing to drop the kids off so I could make my 8am meeting, in London for work, and there was no answer at the door. The girls had run ahead to knock the door and give my Mum a head start in answering it, so I could literally throw the kids in the doorway and run. Usually she was waiting for us, this time nothing. Instinctively I knew something was wrong, and I was right.

She had had a stroke that morning and was no longer physically able to look after my kids. With only one child at school, and the costs of hiring a childminder being far beyond what my single salary could stretch to - I was officially unemployable.

This was long before the days of COVID, or flexible working options were available, and I was instantly out of a job, after explaining my dilemma to my boss.

10 years dedicated to a career, which saw me graduate from my Master's degree pregnant with my second child, and sacrificing countless hours travelling and being away from my kids, was gone overnight.

At the time, the opportunities to work for yourself were scarce. Social media was limited to Facebook, which was mainly used for updating your followers on your lunchtime decisions and uploading your drunk selfies from the weekend. It wasn't yet the money-making opportunity that it is Today.

So again, I found myself starting from zero, when I had to sell my house, the only source of safety I had ever had in life, to buy my first business. I relocated myself and my young family without any support, partner, or friends, to another part of the country hours away, to start my entrepreneurial journey.

Becoming my own boss was a baptism of fire. I had bought a 'turnkey' business, which is one that is already established and allegedly earning a profit. I thought this would be my safest bet, as genuinely I didn't have any clue about how to run a business. On my first day however, after realising that the math wasn't mathing on the accounts that I had been given, it became very clear that I had been sold a sinking ship, with little hope of redemption.

With 3 young kids to support, no way back to my previous life and absolutely no Plan B, I had to get to work. This involved putting my ego, fear and any opportunity for failure to one side. I also had to confront my childhood trauma and self-sabotaging traits head on and unlearn everything, that I thought I knew about who I was. Up until this point, I had been a somewhat rebellious, people pleasing chameleon, who tied myself up in knots trying to make others happy. I never put myself first, I didn't advocate for my needs, I was a pushover, and people took advantage of my need for acceptance, day in and day out. Nothing about that version of me, set me up to run a successful business, so I had to adapt and evolve into a new version quickly.

Friends and family told me that I'd changed, and I was exiled from the communities and friendship groups that I had grown up in. As much as it felt like another betrayal at the time, I now know that it was The Universe having my back. I knew I had changed – that was the point and I no longer wanted to be stuck 'in the matrix' and going through the motions of life. I had to change for the sake of my kids, my commitments and my inner badass that had always been inside of me, so that I can unleash my full potential. I knew from my childhood observations, that you couldn't have one foot in lack and one foot in abundance, you had to pick a side and commit to your future reality.

In ending my own toxic family patterns with money, I birthed a mission to support other women to do the same. The thing is, your relationship with money is symbolic of what you feel worthy of receiving in all areas of your life, not just in your bank account. In transforming my relationship with money, I uplevelled my personal boundaries, found my voice, my purpose and stopped allowing anyone else to mould me into the version of me that they wanted me to be.

I evolved as an entrepreneur, into a Business Growth Strategist and Mentor for women. I had a clear line of sight between stepping into your financial power as a woman in business, and ultimately having the means, resources, and autonomy to live life entirely on your own terms.

I have since supported thousands of women globally throughout my career in mentorship and coaching, to create six and seven figure empires, in the most sustainable and aligned ways. I teach my clients how to leverage their time, energy and money, to get the most bang for their buck in their own heart-led businesses.

I have achieved award-winning success, and incredible professional and personal highs. I have been featured in prestigious magazines such as GQ, Glamour, Stylist Magazine, The Successful Founder, The Female CEO, written articles for The Daily Mail and was even interviewed on Fox News in Florida as a 'Woman of Influence'. I have travelled the world attending transformational retreats and leadership conferences, investing nearly six figures into my own personal development. I am a trusted advisor and strategist to other 7 and 8 figure women in business. I am a UN delegate, championing the advancements of women's rights across the globe, and I make sure no woman ever leaves money on the table again. All of this has been achieved while largely solo raising 5 small humans, who are all incredibly good people, and enjoying the flexibility to be present with them, and even homeschool my oldest Daughter.

And I'm just getting started.

My mission is simple, to support tens of 1000s of women to step into their most financially empowered self, so that they can live a life better than their wildest dreams, entirely on their own terms.

Forget realistic success, societal norms and being like everyone else. The women I work with are trailblazers, who no longer allow themselves to dim their light or play small. They are industry leaders and disrupters who stand up for their beliefs and want to make the world a better place. They know they are meant for big things, and that they didn't come this far in life, to only come this far. They are icons in the making, and I am honoured to be supporting them on their journey, in whatever way that I can.

Because when good women, make good money and wield economic power, they do good things, and the world becomes a better place.

My intention for this book is to plant seeds of awareness about money, that will create shifts in the moment, and throughout your next financial evolution, as the seeds begin to take root and flourish. I want this to act as a guide, that you can utilise whenever something comes up for you, to move you through resistance, and form part of your essential self-development toolkit. I hope that you pass this on to girlfriends, clients, and business connections so it can become a movement and bring forward a new wave of kickass, financially abundant, powerhouse female entrepreneurs who never settle for anything less than they deserve.

Throughout these chapters I will share with you all the things that you need to learn and unlearn to unleash your inner Wealthy Woman. I will explain why you are energetically stuck at your current income level, and the steps you need to take to unlock your full financial potential and become the baddass CEO of your life and your business, who makes money on repeat.

My approach is, like most things in life, as a Manifesting Generator, Gemini with traits of ADHD (*When you know, you know)*- to throw everything at it! I have subsequently added multiple modalities to my toolkit such as Neurolinguistic Programming (NLP), Psychology, Hypnotherapy, TIMEline Therapy, Emotional Freedom Technique (EFT) and Human Design so that I can transform my client's relationship with money strategically, energetically, emotionally, practically, psychologically and physiologically too.

I bring together, what are often the missing parts, of most client's transformations when it comes to money. Typically, I will see women creating affirmations, setting goals, getting clear on their numbers but missing out on the other fundamental parts of the puzzle. This means they end up having to rely on their conscious willpower alone, without realising that if they don't have a belief system that is in alignment with what they want, believing that they are worthy of receiving more money, and that is safe for them to do so, that they will unconsciously self-sabotage their own attempts at receiving the very thing that they desire most.

The reality is, deep down we all want to be good girls, who feel accepted and liked by our communities and 'tribes', so if you have a goal that becomes in conflict with that, you will resist achieving it at all levels.

It's like having one foot on the gas, and one foot on the break.

My invitation to you, is that you do not let this become *another* money mindset book, that you feel excited to read, but actually never do anything with. The key to creating long-lasting success and true transformation, is to *lean all the way in*, do the work and integrate the lessons you will learn along the way. I will show you how, with clear and intentional action steps at the end of every chapter, so that you can implement and embody your learnings, and finally become the boujee-est, baddest, most abundant version of you – The Wealthy Woman.

The Wealthy Woman is a phrase that I feel encapsulates everything that I am trying to empower my clients to embody.

The Wealthy Woman is confident, she is brave, she trusts herself to make the right decisions and turns *inward* for guidance, instead of seeking the answers and validation *outside* of herself. She is abundant in all areas of her life and knows that sacrifice doesn't need to be part of any formula for success. She surrounds herself with those that lift her up, respect her boundaries, and add to her life in all ways. She invests in her self-care, her health, her business, her own personal growth and development and is also building a mean investment portfolio along the way. She knows that no goal is outside of her reach because she can tap into the full abundance, resourcefulness and resilience that is available to her, to make things happen, whenever she wants. She doesn't compete, she isn't intimidated, she doesn't allow her ego to run the show. She is generous, she gives back and always opens doors for the women who are coming up behind her. She is fun, fabulous, and vibrant. She travels, she has diverse interests and is a great cheerleader to have on your team. Her energy is magnetic. She empowers herself with knowledge. She is intimate with her finances and knows how to spend, invest and save well. She knows the value that she brings to the table, so she doesn't discount her services or lower her expectations. She knows time is an illusion and that she can create quantum leaps whenever she feels called to. She balances masculine and feminine energy in her business intuitively and allows herself to be supported on her journey – she knows she wont get to 7 figures alone! She is purpose driven and has a heart-felt, divinely led mission to serve her clients at the highest possible level. She is committed to mastery. She is not here for social media followers or 'likes', she's here for legacy and next level generational wealth. She is The Wealthy Woman.

No pressure, but we are the generation that will change the game for our daughters, and the generations to come, as we redefine what success looks like, and step into our most empowered, zero-fucks-self.

If you are reading this book, I already know that you also have that inner knowing that you were meant for a life that is a lot more extraordinary than the one that has been previously set out for you.

So, without further ado, lets dive in… Your financial evolution awaits!

CHAPTER 1

The Context - Why It's Harder for Women to Make Money

"Teach her about how money really works, and she can change the world" – Tony Robbins

If you are a woman who grew up in the 90s, this may be hard to hear, and downright offensive to your inner channelled girlband member of the Spice Girls; but it is harder for women to make money, than men, and the statistics support it.

88% of businesses owned by women will never make six figures in revenue, let alone seven. Whilst the highly coveted £10k month, sounds like a lot of money, the harsh truth is that after taxes and expenses, you are still only one unexpected bill from a complete financial shit-show. I still remember in my corporate days as a HR Manager, to earn six figures in income you would literally need to be the owner of the company or part of the board of Directors.

Nowadays, whilst six figures are certainly more achievable than ever, it's still quite simply not enough, to experience true financial freedom, build wealth or wield economic power.

Female-led businesses are only 44% of the size of male-led businesses on average, in terms of their contribution to the economy. Male SMEs are also five times more likely to scale up to £1million turnover than female SMEs. This means that we can't employ teams, set up charitable initiatives, free ourselves up from the day to day running of our business, or affect change in any meaningful way.

In other words - we can't change the world, we're too goddamn busy!

Our businesses are continually stuck at the survival level of success, rather than thriving. This fight or flight response to entrepreneurship, leaves us draining our adrenals, and is the ultimate killer of creativity and innovation.

I have personally witnessed countless peers in the coaching space who are projecting success on their socials but are secretly hustling month to month to find their next clients, with ad spends that suck out all of their hard earned profits, and are only one failed launch away from financial jeopardy.

Women also have the highest start up and close rate of businesses, which prevents us from getting traction in any particular marketplace or reaching our true financial potential. I believe that is because women most commonly cite 'necessity' rather than 'opportunity' as a motivation, when starting a business, and so aren't setting themselves up for long lasting success. Just as I had to pivot, when my Mum became sick, and childcare was too expensive for my kids, most women are in the same boat. They aren't focussed on building huge empires, they literally just want flexibility to fulfil their other commitments i.e., child and family caring responsibilities. Without the entrepreneurial vision to fuel their expansion plans, they are more likely to build their business on a shoestring which is a mental feat of resourcefulness and doesn't lend itself to long-term sustainable success.

How did we get here?

Nothing about you is basic or simple, therefore the answer to this question is also multi-layered and diverse as well.

The Neuroscience

Women's brains are wired to be more risk-adverse than men's, because of our heightened sensitivity towards foreseeing loss. I have seen many women unintentionally creating their own upper limits, because they aren't prepared to 'go all in' on their businesses.

They prefer to settle instead for pocket money side hustles, because they are not confident in their ability to achieve more.

When working in Human Resources in my corporate job, I saw this first hand, how women would earn significantly less than their male counterparts. Surprisingly, this wasn't always due to the glaringly obvious gender pay gap, that was common practice in most of the industries that I worked in. It was because, men were far more likely to put themselves out there, and apply for promotions, when they became available. Women would be terrified of rejection, so they would coast along in jobs that they could do with their eyes closed instead.

It's reported that men only need to be 60% confident in their ability to perform a role, to throw their 'hat in the ring' and apply for the job, perceiving failure as no big deal. Women however need to be 100% sure that they have the attributes and experience needed, before they will apply. They equally don't apply for as many jobs, and are therefore putting their eggs, in far fewer baskets.

This risk aversion plays out time and time again in business, when women refrain from taking bold audacious, action towards their goals, preferring instead to be 'realistic' or conservative in their expectations and actions, so they don't lose too much if they don't succeed. This absolutely affects their earning potential as a result. They are also less likely to make financial investments, even though statistically we are more likely to make greater returns on long-term investments.

Where men prefer the dopamine hit from high stakes investments, preferring to 'put it all on black' or stay glued to their phone for updates on their day trades, women are better at identifying investments that have opportunities for long-term returns and growth.

Societal Conditioning

Society loves to place expectations on a woman. As a mother, I have experienced this many times as people tell me I am working 'too hard' and doing too much for someone with a young family. My own Mum would often tell me to sit out and bide my time, so I could be in service to my kids, and then try again at launching my own business when they were older.

The reality is, there has never been a more unique time to be a woman. We no longer must choose between having a family, being good partners, daughters, friends, and family members, and having a successful business. We can *have* it all, but only if we stop trying to *do* it all.

I now get to earn more money than ever, whilst fulfilling my soul's purpose.
And I get to be super present with my kids and available for every moment and milestone.
And I get to work the hours I want, deliver the offers and services that I want, and only work with the highly coveted Unicorn clients that I want.
And I get to pay it forward and support the charitable initiatives that I want, treat family members, employ other incredible women in my team, and be the change that I want to see in the coaching space.

I am so incredibly grateful for this opportunity, and I don't intend to waste it, or lowball my potential.

I often wonder how different my upbringing would have been, if my Mum had had the same opportunities to create a second income from her phone, and whether that would have given her the confidence and the income needed to save our home and keep our family together. The ripple effect of the time in which we lived, has echoed throughout my life, and it would have done the same for my kids, if I hadn't taken such a proactive approach in ensuring that our toxic family cycles with money ended with me.

In addition to the stereotypical roles and expectation that we bend to as women, we are also less likely to:

- Have entrepreneurial role models to shortcut our success, open doors, show us the way, or encourage us on our journey.
- Have a solid financial or entrepreneurial education, instead being pushed into more creative, supporting, and caring careers instead.
- Have the time needed to work on our business and give it the energy it deserves to make it a success, without the fear of failing in other areas of our lives. God forbid that our toilet is not Instagram worthy and gleaming.
- Invest in ourselves to make our business a success. We are less likely to invest in software, teams, advertising or mentors that could make us much more money in the long run.
- Advocate for the support we need at home, to optimise our time and energy. Hello, my name is Rebecca, and I was the 'Martyr Mum' who believed she needed to do everything alone, to be all things to all people and prided myself on how many projects I could multitask at a time. I was even the Chair of the PTA, of a school at which I no longer had any children at, because I didn't trust anyone else enough to pass the baton on to. Don't be the 'Martyr Mum'. It will absolutely cost you money in the long run.

Ancestral Wounds

Through the study of Epigenetics, we can prove that fears, phobias, and traumas can be passed down through our DNA, from our ancestors. This is called Transgenerational Epigenetic Inheritance and is intended to keep you safe, by making you fear certain things that have caused trauma to your past relatives, without even necessarily knowing why.

In spiritual communities, this is commonly known as The Witches Wound, which is a collective intergenerational psychic wound that has scarred women for centuries.

Do you ever feel uncomfortable speaking out, against others, or up for yourself and your needs?

Do you feel threatened when you consider being your most authentic self-online, to market your business, and would rather hide behind a carefully curated 'persona' instead?

Do actions in your industry grate on your personal values, but you fall in line with the status quo, because you don't want to be an outcast from your peers, face a negative backlash online or go against tried and tested approaches for success?

I see this so commonly amongst coaches in the online space who believe they need to project a certain image online, to be taken seriously. They don't feel like being their true self is enough, or safe for them to express, so they dim their light, play small, mimic more successful coaches or otherwise avoid really being 'seen' instead. This results in a one dimensional, cookie cutter, vanilla version of them that does little to inspire quick action, or investment from their audience.

This collective trauma wound has been passed down through many generations amongst women, because of the persecution that we have historically faced for being different or unique. Only 300 years ago, women were still being burned as witches for these very reasons, and yet iterations of this persecution still exist Today. Women are still facing judgement and expectation of how they should look, what they should do with their lives, their bodies, and the masks that they need to wear, to be accepted by society. This presents itself in the women who join my wealth activation program – The Wealthy Woman Academy, as an irrational fear of going live on their social media pages, a need to be perfect before taking action, and a fear of negative feedback online. Fully owning their gifts and their light, is one of the first areas that we work on inside the academy,

This is because your desire to be seen as a 'good girl' who is liked by others, is seriously costing you money and meaning that you are leaving money every day on the table, as you blend into the background and succumb to the noise of the online space and social media. By embracing and owning your voice, your views and your values, you stand out online, and easily set yourself apart from any perceived competition. You call in your dream client, who feels seen and heard by your content, and create a community like no other. No one else has the same connection to your work as you, no one else can serve your clients in the way that you can, no one else has the same unique gifts as you, or can show up with the same passion and conviction – and that, Queen, is your superpower.

If you want to dive deeper into this concept, the book *'Heal the Witch Wound; Reclaim Your Magic and Step Into Your Power' by Celest Larsen* can help you with this.

Governmental Bias

When my Mum had her stroke, and I realised that I was suddenly unemployable, and in need of a more flexible income ASAP, I tried to initially release equity and remortgage my house so that I could remain on the property ladder. After so much sacrifice to even be able to buy my own home in the first place, I didn't want to lose everything that I had worked so hard for. I was shocked however when my request to remortgage my home, was denied, because I was a single parent and considered too much of a risk. Even though I had had a mortgage since I was 18, had hundreds of thousands of pounds in equity in my home, and a history of being a reliable person with a good career behind me. My only choice was to sell my house and buy my business outright.

It didn't even occur to me at the time to try and borrow the money needed or raise investment, because I didn't even know that these were available options. I didn't have anyone in my corner, who was wealth building or astute when it came to finances and investments. I was on my own. Even if I had applied however, the reality is that only 2% of Venture Capital funding ever goes to female-led businesses anyway so my chance of success would have been minimal to say the least.

Why is this a problem?

As entrepreneurs, we are solution providers. The less money you earn, the less likely you are to grow a team, invest in marketing, have access to higher level strategies and mentors so the less clients you end up serving, and the less the world becomes a better place.

Women who make good money, do good things with it, as we are also statistically more likely to donate to charitable causes than men. We are also less empowered to impact change and shape our industries for the better, when we are barely surviving ourselves.

We are not able to grows teams and display leadership that feels more aligned with how we want the world to be, we cannot be the change we want to see in the world when we are just scratching the surface of what we are capable of.

The moral of the story is that the world needs you to be a wealthy woman, and everyone wins when you do.

MINDSET

CHAPTER 2

Why We All Want to Be Good Girls, And Why That's Costing You Money

---

"There are people who have money, and there are people who are rich" – Coco Chanel

If I said to you, would you like more money? Your conscious thought would be "erm yes please", but unconsciously there would be a lot more factoring into that response.

Here's why...

Our brains have only evolved a small percentage since Caveman days (up to 10%), and by nature we are social creatures who want to be part of a tribe or heard. This is because back in the day, there was quite literally strength in numbers, and being part of a tribe gave us the greatest odds of survival, when faced with harsh winters and sabre-toothed tigers. Our brains have a clear line of sight between community and safety, even though thankfully, with the development of apps such as Ubur eats, you are very unlikely to starve if you can't cook, and being eaten by tigers on your way to work is no longer a thing.

This ingrained habit of needing social acceptance is hard to shake, as it's directly connected to one of our brain's primary goals to keep us safe and ensure the survival of our species.

Creating safety around receiving more money, is the first thing you must master, to not only energetically become a match to welcoming more money into your life, but also be able to keep it. 70% of lottery winners lose their winnings within the first few years, because they don't have a belief system that tells them it's safe for them to have that sort of money. They unconsciously self-sabotage and reject their wealth. When you then add in all the other elements contained within this book, such as family pressure to stay humble and be a 'good person', along with feelings of unworthiness of their newfound success, it's no wonder why they end up back at zero. They give their money away, make poor investment decisions or spend it like they stole it. I had a similar experience when creating my first six-figure business as a Barber Shop owner, after leaving my corporate career.

Consciously I wanted to make enough money to replace my salary and enjoy time freedom and flexibility with my children.

Unconsciously I had a belief system, and past experiences, that told me that no-one would love me unless I spent money on them. I was then generous to a fault and gave anyone who wanted one, a job in my shop, usually paying more than industry averages, as I wanted to be seen to be a 'nice' person and promote loyalty amongst my staff. In business, whether your staff like you or not, you are still the boss, and no amount of generous pay or commission will form a connection that runs deeper than that. I once had a meeting with my Accountant, that informed me that the amount of money I spent each week on buying my staff coffee, was downright excessive, and not the tax-deductible expense that I thought it was. I was taking money out of my profit margin every day that I tried to buy my staff's respect.

I have countless clients who have had similar experiences, whether it's through chronically undercharging for their services, overdelivering to a point of burn out, or leaving money on the table daily in their business, so as not to seem too 'salesy'. I believe this is why only 2% of female-owned businesses ever hit 7 figures in revenue. You might think, well I would be happy with much less income in my business, but the reality is, to make real change in this world, you need to make a sizeable income to do so. (More on this later).

Are you the woman, who breaks out into a sweat when the cheque comes for dinner or coffee, when dining with friends? Would you rather tackle the waitress for the bill, so that you can pay it first, so as not to get involved in any awkward conversations about who paid last time?

Maybe you buy thoughtful gifts for others, but the same level of care and intention, never seems to come back your way?

Maybe you have held back on charging the prices you actually want or need, in order to create a sustainable business, because you either fear no one will be able to pay those prices, or worry that people will think of you as greedy?

Yes, self-sabotage can form many sneaky disguises, such as telling you that you don't 'need' lots of money right now, or that you don't want to be like 'those' business owners, who only care about the money and not their clients. This is because your brain wants to keep you safe from perceived negative consequences, of not being liked by your tribe.

Consciously and logically, you may think more money would equal access to better healthcare, better quality food, and more time freedom to exercise, take nice trips and essentially live your best life. You would be right, but what might surprise you to know is that your conscious thoughts are only responsible for 5% of your overall thoughts and behaviours. According to Sigmund Freud, a famous neurologist, your brain is made up of 3 parts, which resemble the image of an iceberg.

The first part is where your conscious thoughts and perceptions are stored, driven by the beliefs and experiences that live within the unconscious part of your brain.

The second part is the preconscious part of your brain, which has access to memories and knowledge that you could access with intention and focus. I personally seem to lack this ability, as I am the woman that often walks into a room without remembering why I was there, it could be however because I am also an overstimulated Mum of 5 who love to keep me busy!

The largest section, however, is the unconscious or subconscious part of your brain. This is where your beliefs, morals, fears, traumas, past experiences, selfish desires live, and where your bodily operations are executed. It's this part, which is ultimately running the show, when it comes to your thoughts, beliefs and actions which are therefore creating your reality when it comes to money.

So, if you aren't happy with the number of zeros in your bank account right now, chances are you have an unconscious belief system that is out of alignment with the very thing that you want – more money.

When I have been interviewed for press articles, I am often asked, what is the number one thing that is keeping people stuck at their current income level and I answer without a moment's hesitation – 'Their need to be liked, is keeping them broke'.

Journal Prompts

Throughout this book, I will share with you powerful journal prompts, that you can use to lean further into the concepts that I'm sharing. If you aren't used to journalling, for self-development, you may feel a sudden urge to eyeroll, but bear with me. Studies have shown many positive benefits of journalling as a daily practice for success, here are some of the reasons that using this powerful practice can make you richer, in more ways than one:

1 – Writing down your thoughts, feelings and experiences creates a deeper sense of self-awareness, which is a must in transforming your relationship with money. If you cannot become more aware of your patterns, triggers, and unconscious

beliefs, you cannot change them, so they will continue to have an influence over your behaviour.

2 – By nature, I am a solution driven person. If you have a boyfriend who is continually not treating you well, I am not the friend to come to when you want to moan and eat copious amounts of ice-cream. I am the friend you come to however, when you are finally ready to move on, and want a next-steps plan of action. You can also bring ice-cream. Taking over the world, making bold changes and changing the game entirely, always requires a lot of energy, so ice-cream is always a plus.

Journalling daily can access creative parts of your brain, that can unlock new and innovative solutions to any problem. When writing about any challenges you are facing, such as 'How can I make more money in my business right now?', you naturally begin to explore different perspectives, consider possible solutions and gain insights that might not have surfaced without the writing process. When you give your brain a question, it wants to find an answer, so put it to work!

3 – Journalling is a great emotional release. One of the things that I will share throughout this book, is how you can hold onto past traumas around money, physically in your body. This invokes a visceral response that will lower your vibrations, and make your whole body want to run away from repeating past mistakes. When you can neutralise that response, through emotional releases, you begin to change the game entirely with money. It no longer has the energetic hold over your unconscious. Journalling supports this process by allowing you to process past trauma and emotions, let them go, reduce the stress response, and promote much needed healing.

4 – It allows you to witness your own evolution and personal growth. Here's the thing, with every new level of income and situation around money, there will be a new layer of personal growth that needs to be mastered, to avoid falling back into old habits and patterns of behaviours. New level, new devil.

Your financial evolution is not a one and done. It's a continual uplevel, like most relationships, that will continue to strengthen and flourish over time. The more that you can witness and document this growth, the more you reclaim the power that money has over your life, and the more empowered you become, as you celebrate every win and milestone. The more you remind yourself, that you can do hard things, even when they are scary, create incredible success without any guarantees to back you, the more you remind yourself what a badass you are.

5 – Journalling can make you rich, by accessing creative parts of your brain, that can act as a continual source of innovation and inspiration for your life and

business. As women we already have access to divine feminine, creative energy that we can tap into at any point. The problem is, we are conditioned to shut it down, looking outside of ourselves instead for solutions and answers.

We look to others to model what 'success' looks like and try and emulate their results. This leaves a massive amount of innovation and originality on the table, that could give you additional ways to make money in your business, serve your clients and truly stand out online with something that others have not yet seen before.

I believe a lack of these basic business skills is a huge part of why most businesses fail. The owners lack the ability to pivot, and move, in response to consumer trends and needs. They find one thing that works and ride it so hard until the energy dissipates, like an exhausted horse put out pasture. Journalling can help you to gain fresh perspectives on existing challenges, generate new ideas and explore creative solutions that will ultimately lead to generating more money inside and outside of your business.

With all this being said, you are hopefully now a huge fan of journalling and/or at least willing to give it a go and tackle the first prompts below. These will give you a chance to really integrate the concepts that you are learning throughout this book, awareness is key. When you know better, you do better!

1 - When you think of having more money, and stepping into your Wealthy Woman identity, what sacrifices to your personality, do you believe you will need to make, to get there?

2 - How have you let the fear of not being liked, hold you back from making or receiving more money?

3 - What is your perception of a wealthy woman and how she treats others?

4 - How have others' opinions of wealthy people, shaped your behaviour in the past?

CHAPTER 3

Why You Don't Really Want to Be Rich

"Create the highest, grandest vision possible for your life, because you become what you believe" – Oprah Winfrey

Your beliefs about what is 'safe' for you to receive, and what you are worthy of receiving, is determining your current reality with money. As I've said before, you may 'consciously' want more money, but if your belief system tells you, it's bad, wrong, or unsafe for you to actually have more money, you will reject that money at every turn.

So how do you know what your beliefs are about money, if you aren't consciously aware of them? It's a dilemma I sat with, when I finally decided that I had had enough of my continual financial rollercoaster and trying to rationalise my own BS. I realised, I was perfectly capable and comfortable with making and receiving money. The moment things felt 'too good' however, I would start to feel uncomfortable and be continually waiting for the shoe to drop, and for someone to come and take it away from me.

This caused me to overspend, be generous to a fault and move into a 'I better enjoy it while it lasts' mindset. I didn't realise that I had some seriously negative beliefs about money, and the damage I believed it had caused me and my family over the years. I was blaming money, as if it was a person, and secretly resenting it every time it showed up, with the belief that it wouldn't stick around long, so I better enjoy it while it lasted. I believed 'the tax man will take it anyway' and the people that created long-lasting wealth were somehow penny pinching, selfish hoarders who obviously didn't care about making the world a better place.

I had things so wrong on every level, it was no wonder that I couldn't seem to keep hold of money for long, before ending back up at zero again. Unconsciously I resented every part of it and self-sabotaged at every turn! The first step in truly transforming my relationship with money, was to understand where these beliefs had even come from in the first place.

There was never a more telling moment, than when I heard a sentence come out of my own mouth, that could have actually been out of the mouth of my Mum. I was advising a friend who was buying her house with her boyfriend, that she should always ensure that she had her own money, separate from that of her partner.

I uttered the immortal words, that my Mum used many times to advise me in the same position – '*never let the left hand know what the right hand is doing*'. As these words left my mouth, I stopped in my tracks. My mum had always instilled in me the belief that men could not be trusted, that money doesn't last, and people will only want to be in your energy if they planned to take money away from you. I had mirrored this own lack of trust in others my whole life, by working 3 jobs when my boyfriend at the time could have easily supported me financially. I was regurgitating her views on men, money, and humanity as a whole, and yet this was the first time, that I was making this connection.

So how do your beliefs even become a thing?

Like every good superhero, every woman has a compelling origin story, now it's time to uncover yours.

Your beliefs are formed in early childhood, before the age of 7 when your brain is essentially a walking talking sponge, soaking up all the information around you, so that you can get a lay of the land ASAP, and become an accepted member of your tribe.

I once read a book on the psychology of children, while sunning myself in the Bahamas and I was shocked at just how manipulative tiny humans can be. Did you know that a baby will automatically resemble more of their dad's features than their Mum's as a way of manipulating them into wanting to stay close and protect them? I digress...

When a baby is born it will already have an inherent fear of two things – being dropped (demonstrated by their Moro Reflex (startle reflex), where they will throw out their arms, to support their fall) and loud noises.

They will have these fears from birth, to keep them safe and they will have been passed down to them through their ancestral genetics. Everything else they must learn on the job. To do this, their brains are learning in hyper-speed. They are rapidly creating new neural network connections, which are shaped by every interaction they have. These interactions give them a sense of how things work in the real world, so that they can be accepted by their caregivers and tribe. Think of a brand-new Apple I Phone, fresh out of the box, just waiting to be programmed.

The problem is, they haven't yet cultivated emotional intelligence, due to the lack of their critical faculty function, which doesn't develop until the ages of 10-12, so they are unable to apply logic or context to any situations that they observe.

Your Critical Faculty is the firewall that stands between your conscious and unconscious brain. It stops messages being automatically accepted by your unconscious mind (which is where your beliefs are formed) and gives your conscious mind a chance to reject or distort the information received, by applying logic and context first.

Up until the age of 7 this part is missing. So, anything you see or observe, your brain will automatically accept as truth and apply a meaning to. All without the context or maturity to see them for what they really are.

This is great for parents who want to convince their children that the Easter bunny and Santa are real, without having to discuss the feasibility or logistics, of how Santa is going to get down a chimney that you don't have. It's not so good for a child who is witnessing unhealthy relationships and conversations about money, that then forms part of their foundational belief system.

If you saw your parents arguing about money, you would have applied the very literal meaning that money = arguments, sacrifice, and all-round negative outcomes. Your brain would then decide that money is something that you want to avoid at all costs, so that you don't suffer the same pain.

Equally, if you heard negative stories about wealthy people such as *'the rich get rich while the poor get poor'* you would have also decided, that to be a liked member of your tribe, and a good girl, you most definitely did not want to be one of *THOSE* wealthy people.

I have also had clients inside my Wealthy Woman Academy who came from a very comfortable or wealthy family but felt guilty about being so fortunate, because they could feel the hostility from others as they grew up. They then play small as adults, because they want to remain humble and grateful, because there are always more people out there who are less fortunate.

They also had absent parents, who were working long hours in exchange for that financial security, and they felt resentful towards their sacrifice. A small child is not interested in investment accounts and pension pots, they just want their dad to tuck them in at bedtime. They then sabotaged their own business growth potential because they still remember the sting of the perceived rejection, when their dad was working late *again,* and they don't want to inflict the same pain on their own children. They don't fully appreciate that we are living in a different time, with increased opportunities available to us, so we no longer have to choose between family and wealth – we get to have both, AMEN to that!

I also have clients who had a comfortable family life and felt bad for wanting more for themselves beyond their basic needs and had tried to stay humble and grateful.

I have also spoken to women whose parents had very toxic post-breakup relationships, where the goal was to annoy each other and inflict as much pain as possible. This looked like an absent father refusing to pay child support, to annoy their Mum, but instead implanted the belief that THEY were not worthy of the money instead.

The mind really is a fascinating machine that is responding only to the data it has been programmed with, the good, the bad and the ugly.

Having this awareness, that your beliefs are not always your own, is the first step in reclaiming your power from the ones that do not serve you. The beliefs that undermine your big, heartfelt goals, the ones that keep you small or make you feel bad for wanting a big, extraordinary life. Those are the beliefs that do not serve you, and the big impact you were meant to have in this lifetime. The good thing is, as I have said before, when you know better, you do better and creating awareness is the first step in reprogramming those beliefs, to ones that are going to help you, not hinder you, in pursuit of your next level life.

Journal Prompts:

1 - What is your earliest memory relating to money?

2 - What did you hear and see that relates to money when you were a child?

3 - What was your mother's relationship with money, what did she tell you? What did you witness?

4 - What was your father's relationship with money, what did he tell you? What did you witness?

5 - What were your wider family and community's attitudes towards money?

6 - What did you see on TV about women that were wealthy? (Typically they're depicted as bossy, money grabbing and ruthless, who only became humble and nice, once they had lost their fortune – Shout out to Anne Hathaway in 'The Devil Wears Prada', and Goldie Hawn in 'Overboard')

7 - What are your memories from being a teenager relating to money? (Typically, this is when we start forming our own desires for money)

CHAPTER 4

Turning Up the Heat on Your Wealth Thermostat

"I think my story says that, when women are given the chance and the opportunity, that we can achieve a lot. We deliver" – Sara Blakely

Your current reality with money, is an indication of the temperature of your Wealth Thermostat. This is your energetic maximum and minimum amount of money that you feel safe, and worthy of receiving, before you begin to unconsciously reject it.

Is there an amount of money that you cannot imagine earning less than in your business?

Is there an amount of money that you cannot imagine earning more than, without a serious inner pep talk, and breaking out into a light sweat?

The number between those amounts is known as your Wealth Thermostat.

Take a moment to put your hand on your heart and think of your next level of financial income. What is that number?

Now imagine adding an extra 10%, imagine doubling it, tripling it, and observing how that feels in your body. At what point does the number become so wildly unrealistic that you cannot get behind receiving it? That number is your self-imposed upper limit to your wealth thermostat.

To increase it, you need to do these few things:

- Examine your beliefs about money and identify the ones that are not serving you and are actually unhelpful in the pursuit of wanting more.
- Create safety around receiving that amount of money. That could be by finding evidence of other people that have it, that are still good, happy, heart-led people that you would be happy emulating their success.
- You can also future pace your desire, to remove the fear of the unknown. The more you embody and imagine what it would be like to live the life that you want, the less resistance you will have to receiving it.

Let's apply your Wealth Thermostat to your current experiences with money.

What can you not imagine doing?

Paying your rent, or bills on time?

Maybe you can imagine paying your bills, but you can't imagine having enough left over for luxuries?

Maybe you can pay your bills, and have money for luxuries, but feel bad when you think of those that can't, or aren't as fortunate as you?

What are the feelings that come up for you?

Those feelings, and visceral responses, are setting your energetic minimum and maximum income levels.

As I mentioned at the start of this chapter, you may consciously, have a full body 'yasssss please' to making more money, but if you have a belief system that tells you it is bad or wrong, to want more, here's how it will play out…

Conscious Desire – *You want more money, you're ready, let's go!*

Unconscious Belief – *Rich people are greedy, you can't charge too much, or people will not be able to afford you, and you don't want to leave anyone behind. If you take on more clients, it will mean more tax, less time with loved ones, more stress, more work.*

Feelings and Emotional Experience – *It feels hard to attract clients who want to pay your prices, you feel overwhelmed with the (perceived) amount of work needed to take your business to the next level, maybe you're doing it wrong, everyone else makes it look so easy, this feels hard, you can't be that good. you feel tired and drained.*

Actions (Or No Actions) – *You feel overwhelmed, you put things off till later, you struggle to be consistent, you don't show up with* confidence in what you're selling, you look for the next shiny object, and think 'maybe I'll launch something else instead..'

Outcome – *No client buys in, money is left ALL OVER the table, your confidence is shot to pieces, you experience feast and famine cycles in your business, you feel unable to invest in yourself or a team to grow your business.*

Your belief is then confirmed by the outcome, that you are no good at what you do, people don't like you, making money is hard.

And so the cycle continues…

This cycle breaks my heart, as a Business Mentor, who has seen many incredibly talented female entrepreneurs come and go over my 8 years in business, retreating to corporate, because they couldn't figure out the money piece of their strategy.

At the end of the day, money is just the fuel that is necessary to sustain and grow your business, it isn't an indication of how good or talented you are.

With this new awareness, of how these early childhood beliefs can influence your adult experiences, and therefore your current reality, can you now connect the dots and identify the current beliefs that may be causing you to unconsciously hold back from reaching your full potential?

Take a moment to journal on any of the questions throughout this chapter, that have resonated with you, so that you can unpick them and identify what you are really saying about money, underneath it all.

CHAPTER 5

Neutralising Your Money Traumas

"Many people take no care of their money till they come nearly to the end of it, and others do just the same with their time" – Johann Wolfgang von Goethe

To start the process of creating new beliefs, we need to create space and let some shizzle go!

This section in the book is where you acknowledge and heal your past money traumas, so that you can move forwards without the emotional charge attached to money and create a new financial future. If you don't deal with the shizzle first, you will always have one foot on the gas, and one foot on the break, when it comes to going all in on your financial goals.

One of the things I observed when surrounding myself with wealthy people, was their complete neutrality to it. They didn't obsess or worry about it, night, and day, they saw it as a predictable resource that would be there whenever they needed it instead. Whilst they saw making money as fun, they didn't put it on a pedestal, or rely on it to make them happy.

Even if they had experienced financial losses in the past, they didn't let it define them or believe that they had 'missed their shot', they understood money is an unlimited resource, and that there is always more available to them.

This ability to bounce back from financial losses, without allowing it to knock their confidence or scar them indefinitely, is why there are many reported cases of millionaires who lose it all and make it back in record time.

The thing is everyone has trauma around money. It's inevitable, whether we grew up poor, rich or somewhere in the middle, because trauma is relative.

What might be no biggie to some, could be the end of the world to others, we all have our own shizzle to deal with.

These bad memories and negative emotions around money, will be affecting your financial flow of abundance. They could come from childhood moments where you witnessed your parents arguing about money, this would have formed an association with money and negative consequences.

They could have come from shame around debt, guilt around making a bad investment, worry about times of lack, feeling let down when a payment didn't arrive in time - it all counts!

It could just be that you never got the bike you wanted at Christmas, if it made you feel sad or some kind of way, it's a trauma and a core memory that needs to be healed.

For me, one of my earliest traumas was around a school trip that I was supposed to go on, with my friends but never actually went on as my Stepdad spent the money. Twice.

When my dad passed away, I was given a small inheritance, thanks to the sailors on his ship, that had crowdfunded money for my Sister and I, so that we would never have to miss out on things that my Dad would have otherwise been around to pay for.

The money was saved in a Post office account, which could only be accessed by myself and a parent. Security protocols apparently weren't so tight in the 90s! I remember my Stepdad telling me that I needed to withdraw the £700 needed for the trip, but I wasn't to take the cash to school as it wasn't safe. He would write me a cheque instead. When it became time to take the cheque to school, he told me he no longer had the money. Off I went to the Post Office again, to withdraw a second amount of money. The next day, I was excited to get to school and finally hand my cheque in, ready to secure my place with all of the other girls at school,

I was stopped once again at the door and told not to take it. I still remember the sting of tears and anger that I felt, at the injustice of the situation. I knew, even as a child, that his behaviour was not right, but I was utterly powerless to do anything about it, and that is what ate at me most. I was powerless. I was insignificant. People could use me, take things from me, and I had to accept it, because I was powerless to stop them.

This cycle of powerlessness showed up for me several times, in different guises throughout my life, dressed up as narcissist partners, friends who loved a freebie, staff who overstepped boundaries and clients who wanted my soul, whenever they invested in my programs. I felt powerless to refuse people's requests and expectations of me, because I wanted to be liked and the customer is always, right? Right? Wrong!

I wrote about this recently, that when it comes to business, it's your party and you get to run it how you want to. You can work with the clients that you want to, at the price points that you want to, on the platforms that you want and deliver your offers, products, and services in the way that you want to.

You have all the power, because there are 8 billion people in the world, and you only need a small fraction of those to invest in your services, to have a pretty incredible business. You might as well call in the ones that you actually want to work with!

To really move past all the emotional traumas I had, growing up, and as an adult relating to money, I had to heal, forgive and let go of them. It helped to move energy that had otherwise been stuck in my body, festering away, and sapping my energy. It also helped me to reclaim my power from those that had taken it from me in the past.

Head to my website, www.thefemalepreneurcoach.co.uk/bookresources for an incredible guided meditation to support you with this work.

Without intentionally neutralising your emotional responses to money, trauma can easily manifest into illness in your body, affect the potential of your future, and otherwise cause you to live only half a life, as you hold yourself back from getting hurt again.

For now, here are a few simple practices to support you in healing your money dramas, so that you can remove the energetic holds that they have over you and clear the path of financial abundance to get back into your financial flow again.

Practice Forgiveness

Past circumstances around money, only get to affect your present and future, IF you let them.

You cannot change the past or condone anything that others may have done to you, but you can choose to FORGIVE and RELEASE the emotional hold it has over you. Forgiveness is one of the most empowering self-care practices that you can indulge in. Often people can resist forgiving others that have harmed them (including themselves), because they believe they are accepting what happened or saying it is ok. I believe when you forgive someone who harms harmed you, you are saying that their impact is now so irrelevant to you, they no longer have any power to harm you any further. It's every narcissist's worst nightmare. I once read a quote that said, '*Holding onto resentment is like drinking poison, and expecting the other person to die'*, this really struck a chord in me, and has done with the client's that I have worked with over the years.

I once had an incredible client Sarah, who had been working on her money mindset inside my Academy. She had had an ex-partner who was financially controlling and had left her with mountains of debt. She felt extremely resentful about the debt, that she was having to continue to pay, because it felt so unfair that she was left facing the consequences of *his* actions. She felt annoyed and agitated every time she saw the direct debit leaving her account, and reinforced the message that she couldn't be trusted with money because she had been so bad at picking a partner. She had overlooked red flags, at the early stages of her relationship, because she had been grateful to be with a partner who was seemingly so charming. The relationship quickly turned sour, and she was in over her head, having to justify every purchase, because she was made to feel 'useless with money'. We had a lot to unpack!

Firstly, we needed to get to the root cause of why she had been accepting of this person's behaviour. It had stemmed back to her childhood when her Dad was emotionally unavailable. She had always felt like she needed to fight for his attention and was unworthy of his love. Finding a man who mirrored this behaviour, although upsetting, was familiar to her unconscious, and so she had accepted that these dynamics were ok. We then had to change her energy around the money that was leaving her account each month. She could choose to be angry and resentful towards the bill, which would ultimately lead to her manifesting more situations to be angry and resentful about, or she could choose to be grateful and peaceful instead. She could feel gratitude for the lesson learned, from someone so toxic, about what she was no longer willing to tolerate in her life. She could be grateful that she was able to take care of her bills and commitments and was a person with integrity who always paid her debts. She could also feel peace, that while the debt lingered, the relationship did not and that she was able to move forward with her life, whereas her ex was probably destined to continue to repeat his behaviour for the rest of his life – *who wants to be that guy?*

Finally, we had to work on rebuilding her trust in herself and remind her that she was a smart, capable, empowered woman who could be trusted with money and other big picture decisions.

Every month inside The Wealthy Woman Academy we have a 'Money Date' where we work on forgiveness exercises and get intimate with our finances, identify opportunities for growth and money making and ultimately give ourselves a high five for our badass financial evolution.

My favourite practice is simple, simply take a moment to journal on and write out all the negative experiences you can remember around money.

Go through the list in turn, and consciously choose to find gratitude in the lessons learned and forgive each situation.

Visualise a golden light dissolving the energetic chord (and emotional charge) between you and each situation.

If you want to take this one step further, I use a beautiful Hawaiian practice of reconciliation and forgiveness, called Ho'oponopono with my clients. The intention of the practice is to forgive and reconcile the parts of yourself that have been fractured and find peace within the situation. It's a beautiful self-healing ritual, that I use each month to acknowledge and heal any negative situations around money that have come up for me that month, so that I can get back into my financial flow, without energetic or unconscious obstructions.

When you have your list, you can go through each instance in turn and simply recite the words:

'I'm Sorry, Please Forgive Me' - You are saying 'I am sorry for any part that I played in the situation, and/or for allowing it to still have a hold over me'. You are not accepting the part of the other person, just being accountable for your own actions and emotions.

'I Love You' – In this moment you are saying to yourself, and The Universe, I love you, regardless of past mistakes, bad things that happened, I love you. You can even be saying to the situation, I love you for the lesson that this moment created, and the strength I now have as an outcome.

'Thank You' – There is a lesson and a blessing in 99.9% of bad situations, and in this moment, you are acknowledging that. You also expressing gratitude at the fact that this will be no longer be a thing for you, in advance of it clearing.

You have survived 100% of your worst days, and I have no doubt that you are a Bad B*tch because of them. I truly believe that I would not have the layers, the depth, the empathy, or a mission so big, that I do today if I had not been through so much shizzle as a child.

If that means I now get to serve at a higher level, and in some small way, make the world a better place, because of the strength, emotional intelligence, and fortitude that I have now created, I am grateful.

Reframe

If you struggle to go straight to forgiveness, try to reframe your negative situations around money instead.

If you made a bad investment, or racked up a lot of debt - reframe the belief you have that what happened was something bad and find a positive lesson instead.

I.e., 'I am the kind of person that follows me heart, goes all in and is willing to pay money for the things that feel are right at the time'.

'Thank you for the lesson of overspending, I now know I won't ever repeat this pattern again'.

'Yes, that guy was a D*ck but I am so proud of my resilience and won't ever let anyone take advantage again'.

Emotional Freedom Technique (EFT)

EFT or tapping, removes the emotional charge from the negative situation, disperses the stuck energy around the trauma, and anchors in positive reframes. It works in the same way as Chinese acupuncture, by working with the energy meridian points in your body and releasing stuck energy.

I have found it to be truly powerful, when used with my clients, and can be applied to any situation where you feel uneasy, stuck, or anxious. The best part is, it is a simple technique, that you can use on yourself, from the comfort of your own home.

It involves tapping on specific pressure points on your body, primarily on your head, face, chest, and hand, in a particular sequence, while focussing on the issue or memory that you want to release.

I will explain the process in basic terms, but if you would like a visual demonstration, head to the resources section on my website, www.thefemalepreneurcoach.co.uk/bookresources where I take you through the entire cycle.

- **Step 1 – Identify the issue.**
  Think about the problem or belief that you wish to resolve. Only focus on one thing at a time. I.e., a belief that people will not buy your offers.

- **Step 2 – Test the intensity of this feeling.**
Rank it using a score from 0-10, with 10 being the most unshakeable feeling that literally feels gut wrenching in your body.

- **Step 3 – The Setup**
Tapping is completed in rounds or cycles. Start every cycle with a setup on the Karate chop point on your hand, which is the centre of the fleshy part of your outer hand (it doesn't matter whether you are left or right-handed).

Create a succinct phrase that encapsulates the belief or feeling that you wish to shift. It acknowledges your issue, whilst also conveying self-acceptance and love in the process. I.e., "Even though I worry that people will not buy my offers, I still totally love and accept myself".

- **4 – The Sequence**
Tap in sequence on the following parts of your body, while repeating the set-up phrase, over and over:

Top of your head (often known as your Crown Chakra)

Beginning of your eyebrow (the beginning of the brow, just above and to the side of your nose)

Side of your eye (on the bone at the outside corner of your eye)

Under your eye (on the bone underneath your eye)

Under your nose (at the point between your nose and upper lip)

On your chin

On your collarbone (where your breastbone (sternum), collarbone, and first rib intersect)

Under your arm (at the side of your body, where your bra-strap would sit)

When tapping, use two or more fingertips and repeat the tap approximately five times on each point.

Do one complete cycle, and then finally

5. Test the intensity again

Using the 0-10 scale, rank the intensity of the emotion again, to see if it has reduced. The goal isn't always to get to zero, but to bring your emotions further down the scale. You can also do another round, and tap IN positive affirmations, to end your cycle on a positive note.

I use this technique with my clients and my children, for all sort of issues, so that they can learn to self-regulate their emotions.

When you can see firsthand, how you have the power to change your physical and emotional state, as opposed to being at the mercy of the stimulus of the outside world, the whole game changes entirely.

Hypnosis & TIMEline Therapy

Sometimes you aren't even consciously aware of your trauma, and it may even be from generations before you! Hypnosis and TIMEline Therapy are another 2 incredible tools that I use with my clients to get to the root cause of their money issues, so that they can clear them and make way for new abundance.

They both work by getting you to a super relaxed state, so that you can bypass the conscious part of your brain and speak directly to the unconscious part instead.

This can give you valuable insights and ensure that any positive reprogramming that you want to add in, like more empowering beliefs are more likely to be accepted, because of your brain's relaxed state. It is less likely to reject the suggestions made.

For powerful hypnosis audios, please head to the resources section of my website www.thefemalepreneurcoach.co.uk/bookresources.

Rescripting Your Financial Future

This exercise is powerful at taking all your past negative experiences, and reframing them in a positive way, to rewrite your financial future.

Instead of being a 'victim' of financial trauma, you get to be a hero in your own story, who has overcome adversity to achieve incredible success. This supports you in identifying more with the future, most empowered Wealthy Woman version of you, who has layers of experience and wisdom under their belt, rather than a victim who is still being affected by past setbacks.

Take a moment now to journal out and rewrite your financial future.

Journal Prompt:

Using the table below as a guide, what is your money story now going to be?

Worn Out Woman Money Story	Wealthy Woman Money Story
The world is unfair, there is no point in trying to improve my situation because everything is always against me	The world is unfair, but I am going to make it better.
I have made so many bad financial decisions and will never get out of debt. I feel so ashamed and guilty.	It's never too late for me to turn my situation around, now I know better, I can do better.
It's too late for me to start investing in my future. I should have done this years ago when I had so much more money.	Years ago, would have been the perfect time to have started investing, Today is the second most perfect time to start investing.
Having my own business feels risky, and making money feels hard, I don't think I am good enough to make this work.	I am resourceful and scrappy. I will make it work because I am good enough to make it work. If I don't know how to do something, I will find someone who can help me figure it out.
I'll always be terrible with money	My future is what I decide to make it. My past does not determine the potential of my future.
I'm not clever enough to make big money or build wealth.	Making money and creating wealth is a skill that I can learn.

This money clearing and forgiveness work needs to be part of your continual money maintenance practices, as with every new level of income, or situation around money, there is always a new devil (or unhelpful belief) waiting to block you.

Again, think of these unhelpful beliefs as an overprotective mother who wants to keep you safe, and send your unconscious brain so much love and compassion. You are not broken, you don't need to be fixed, but you can always expand and grow into your next level, so committing to this work as a weekly, monthly practice is a really great way at ensuring that YOU do not become the block to your own success.

CHAPTER 6

Reprogramming Your Mindset for Success

"Successful people make money. It's not that people who make money become successful, but that successful people attract money. They bring success to what they do" – Wayne Dyer

We used to think that 'old dogs can't learn new tricks', but neuroscience has proved that not only, thanks to neuroplasticity, can our brains learn new things, at any age, we can also evolve into totally new ways of thinking, behaving and BEING too.

Dr Joe Dispenza is one of my all-time favourite authors and reading his book *'How to Breaking The Habit of Being Yourself'* was a pivotal moment in my self-development journey. In the book he shares how you can change your entire personality and repetitive thoughts, to then change your reality.

Growing up, I was surrounded by people who identified with their personality traits. They would say that they were an anxious person, a shy person, someone who was not confident. They wore those traits as part of their basic identity, and it controlled their perception of what they would be able to achieve in life.

When I worked in corporate, before I had 'awoken', thanks to my personal development journey, I was a very different version of the woman who sits here writing this book Today. I was a people pleaser, a hard worker to a point of martyrdom and someone who struggled to say no to the demands of others.

My second baby was nearly born breach, because my excessive travel, and time spent in my car, during the final stage of my pregnancy, had forced her up and under my ribs. I had a narcissistic boss at the time, who tried to force me into early maternity leave, by sending me on ridiculous errands.

I once travelled 9 hours for a 20-minute meeting in Devon, in the middle of severe floods that were being reported on the news, 2 weeks before my due date, because my boss could instruct me to do so.

I didn't feel that I could say no, because she was my boss, and I couldn't afford to go on maternity leave early, as it would mean less time with the baby once she was here. I still remember my partner at the time, who worked at the same company, arguing with me that, if I went into labour, I would be stuck in one of the remotest parts of the country, in the middle of flooding and be having the baby, who may be breach, alone.

I truly believed I was powerless in that situation and felt anxious every minute that I was gone. After a two-day labour with my first child, I was comforted however that I would have time to get myself home if I needed to.

The Universe had my back during my pregnancy because I ended up going into spontaneous labour a few weeks later, delivering the baby start to finish in just 20 minutes, and nearly gave birth in the car.

I am so grateful that it didn't happen while I was alone and stuck in the middle of nowhere. My Guardian Angels were absolutely looking out for me, and the baby, in that moment.

Angels are spiritual beings that are here for your protection, that you can call on in times of need. They embody unconditional love, wisdom and protection and work through your intuition, to guide you away from dangerous situations.

Unexpectedly becoming my own boss, really was the awakening of my fullest potential, not only in terms of capability, skillset, and creativity, but also as a woman. Now, I am stronger and ready to speak out about injustices and toxic behaviour that I see in the online space, and advocate for my clients. My personality has evolved into a whole new way of being and this is because of a few things:

1 - I cultivated radical self-awareness.

Your brain is made up of billions of neurons, that are responsible for creating your thoughts and behaviours. Your brain will receive a stimulus and you will then respond accordingly. Thanks to the discovery of neuroplasticity, we now know that we can rewire our brains to respond in new, more helpful ways.

The first step is creating radical self-awareness around the current thoughts and responses that are not serving you.

If you feel triggered by someone else's success, rather than feeling bad for expressing judgement, ask yourself questions around why it is making you respond in that way? Is there a belief that is making you feel some kind of way, about your own potential, at achieving the same level of success?

Where did this belief come from?

Is it actually true?

*How is it serving you to continue believing that this belief is true? (*In NLP terms, we call this a secondary gain i.e. a positive outcome from staying stuck. I.e. If I don't really go all in on my business, and it doesn't work out, I wont feel that bad because I didn't really try or, if I stay hidden on social media, then I wont have to deal with negative trolls on the internet, who might not agree with my views or if I don't earn too much, I won't have to pay more taxes and deal with complicated accountancy systems)

What would be a more empowering belief instead?

As you move throughout your day, pay attention to the things, people or situations that raise your vibrations, and the things, people or situations that lower it.

Become mindful of the conversations that you are having, and the messages that you are putting out into the world, with your symbolic acts. If you are engaging in conversations that are disparaging about money and going with the low-vibe flow of others, you will see their low-vibe attitudes and actions reflected in your reality.

2 - I committed to daily practices for success.

Our brain learns through repetition, and it takes time to embed new, more positive beliefs about money. It typically takes 21 days to create new habits, and allow your brain's autopilot systems to kick in, so that these thought patterns can become your new ways of being. I have a great podcast episode on how to harness the power of the school run, or your daily commute to work. It shares how these consistent pockets of time, can incrementally create massive shifts in your beliefs, and reprogramming your mindset for success. Head to The Femalepreneur Coach Podcast to listen!

Daily practices can include reading or listening to money mindset books, reciting affirmations, setting positive reminders on your phone, and surrounding yourself with the right people who inspire you and motivate you to want to achieve more.

What practices can you add to your morning or daily routine that will support you in thinking, and acting in new and more empowering ways?

3 - I found evidence that my success was possible.

Another way to break-down your resistance to receiving more money, is to feed your brain the evidence that what you want, is safe, and possible to receive. If your current money goals, feel a little too stretching, and therefore unachievable, set lower goals that feel doable instead. This increases your level of believability and stops your logical brain from causing you to lean out of taking action towards your goals. Not only did I create a ladder of believability by adding mini milestones to my bigger financial goals, I also found evidence of women that had created the same level of success that I desired. Women who were in similar situations to me, with small children at home, who had lots of other things going on too.

When you think about what you want, what are the 'but's that tell you it's not possible? i.e. I would love to earn more money, but.. I have kids so I need to be with them.

I always say to my clients, in the words of Sir Mix-a-lot, "*I like big butts and I cannot lie..*" because those 'buts' give us powerful feedback as to what is keeping you stuck. You can then find the evidence as to why those buts are not as big a deal as you think.

What examples can you find of women in the same position as you, who have created incredible success?

4 - I surrounded myself with the right people who inspired and lifted me up.

Creating an environment for success is a gamechanger. Intuitively, I had already started moving away from people that were very negative about money, but it left me on a lonely island, feeling like no-one understood me anymore. My next step was to find a community of like-minded women who felt more like my tribe. At first, I created my own, on social media, and eventually I began investing in Masterminds and group programs, that put me in the rooms with women who inspired me and motivated me to want more for myself and my legacy. Online and in person networking events are a great way to meet other woman who can form part of your success squad.

Where can you create or find a supportive community that feel more aligned to where you want to go in life?

ENERGETICS

CHAPTER 7

The Frequency of Wealth

"Money is only a tool. It will take you to wherever you wish, but it will not replace you as the driver" – Ayn Rand

You may have heard about a little known booked called The Secret? If you are like me, when that book exploded in 2018, I was hooked. It was published in 2006, but for some reason during the summer of 2018, it was EVERYWHERE!.

I was first introduced by a friend on social media, and from the moment I read it, I was obsessed. The book was written by Rhonda Byrne, after a series of personal and professional setbacks. She was severely depressed and looking for answers, and after reading '*The Science of Getting Rich*', by Wallace D.Wattles, (another one of my favourites) in 1910 she went on a two month voyage of discovery as she traced the origins and principals of the book.

After compiling her research, she pulled together her interpretation of the learnings, from this year and other spiritual leaders and communities, and described them as The Law of Attraction.

Growing up, without a support network to encourage me, books were my saviours. Whether it was for escapism, inspiration, or connection, I have always found a lot of comfort in reading as a way of uplevelling my knowledge, assimilating my thoughts and opinions, feeling seen and understood and really opening my eyes to what was possible for me.

I have so much respect for the writing process, and the transformation that can be created from a few words on a page, which is why I always knew I was meant to write a book. I now encourage my clients, when they want to evolve their relationship with money, to add reading money related books, as part of their daily routine and success habits. Even if you only read a few pages a day, it all makes a difference.

Think how much information (good and bad) you consume daily via social media, the news, radio etc., this is helping to balance that out in a positive way.

More reasons to add daily reading to your success habits:

- Reading reduces stress levels, as you carve out intentional, mindful time without constant interruptions or notifications on your phone or social media.
- Our brains learn through repetition, and continual reinforcement, so committing to just a few pages a day, continues to reinforce new beliefs about money and create safety around your desire for more.
- Exposing yourself to new ways of thinking, and uplevelling your knowledge, increases your comprehension and understanding of the world. This helped me massively in connecting the dots on self-sabotaging patterns of behaviour, that I didn't even realise were a bad thing, before I had that bigger picture awareness. This can be so common for my clients, who don't have the awareness to know, because their beliefs about money are so engrained in their belief system, that *they* are the ones keeping themselves stuck at their current income level. This is why such powerhouses as Billionaire Microsoft Founder, Bill Gates, Billionaire Investor Warren Buffet and even the Queen of all things, Billionaire Oprah Winfrey has her own book club – notice the theme? Leaders are readers, and they make bank by quietening their mind, and focussing on their own personal development through reading.
- Activates the creative parts of your brain and brings forward new ideas and inspiration, that have served me many times in my business to create something exciting, that has paid me back financially. Whether that was a new marketing campaign, a new offer for my audience or just an exciting event I then went on to host, it always comes back to the inspiration I've taken from something I've read and then built on in my own way.

If you don't have the patience for reading, audiobooks and podcasts are great too! Choose whatever works for you and make those pockets of time on the school run, on your journey to work, while making dinner, or walking your dog, work for you and nurture your success mindset.

You can head to the book resources page on my website – www.thefemalepreneurcoach.co.uk/bookresources for a list of my own carefully curated, and personal favourite Money Mindset Books that have supported me on my own Money Evolution journey.

In The Secret, Rhonda talks about The Law of Attraction, and how you can activate your own personal magnetism and power to manifest or call in your heart's desires.

What you might not know however, is that The Law of Attraction is only one of the 12 spiritual Laws of The Universe, that are themed around how the energy of the Universe works. These are essentially the rules of the game, so knowing how to work with the energy puts you ahead of the curve, keeps you in alignment and makes you more likely to manifest what you want.

Not knowing or understanding these laws will see you working against the very Universals laws that are trying to support you.

Working on your money story and the unhelpful beliefs that are blocking the abundance available to you is the first step, mastering the Universal laws is then like throwing gasoline on top.

The 12 spiritual laws are:

1 – The Law of Divine Oneness

This is the main law that governs all things, and states that we are all connected as spiritual beings. There is no separation, no one is better or luckier than someone else, we are all connected and therefore equally likely to succeed. The next time you feel triggered by someone else's success, rather than feeling jealous, feel inspired that if *they* can do it, so can You!

2 – The Law of Vibration

The Law of Vibration states that everything whether tangible or intangible, is made up of energy that vibrates at a specific frequency. From our sofa, pets and friends to our emotions, thoughts and feelings, everything is constantly vibrating. We are all energy in motion. You can only attract into your life, the things, opportunities, and people, that are vibrating at the same frequency.

Have you ever heard the expression, 'when it rains it pours?' – this is the Law of Vibration in action. When you are in a low vibe state, you attract more things that are vibrating at this frequency. When you want to manifest something that is above the frequency of where you currently are, you need to elevate your emotions, perspectives, and actions to that next level too, otherwise those things will pass you by.

Have you ever been stuck in a conversation with an energy vampire before? Those are the people that are super low vibe and literally drain the life out of you when you speak to them.

Do you also have friends that seem to attract continual drama and issues? Every time you speak to them, there is always *something* going wrong.

They are usually stuck in a toxic cycle of misery, or low vibe memories of the past, that only manifests more reasons to be miserable. They need to create awareness around how their thoughts, behaviours and energetic state are continuing to attract more drama, stress, and misery.

Elevating your emotions and energetic states, or raising your frequency, allows you to attract better, opportunities, people, situations and yes money into your life. This is how positive, unexpected things seem to happen, seemingly by magic. Head over to my resources page at
www.thefemalepreneurcoach.co.uk/bookresources to view the frequency scale of emotions. This isn't about walking around in a state of toxic positivity however, we are spiritual beings, who are meant to experience the full range of the emotional spectrum.

It's about having emotional intelligence and self-leadership as a woman, to guide yourself back to thoughts and emotions that serve you, rather than staying stuck or wallowing at the lower end of the scale, when things don't work out.

3 – The Law of Correspondence

This law states that your external reality is a direct reflection of your internal belief system. This law always made sense to me, even before I could get behind the more spiritual principals, as I had witnessed firsthand growing up, how someone's limiting beliefs of themselves or money, would become the self-fulfilling prophesy and be reflected back to them in their current situation. By believing that they were not worthy of receiving more money, or 'lucky break's, they would expect the worst from every situation, so they never went all in on their goals, they overlooked opportunities to make money and they never backed themselves.

My Mum was a classic example of this. She didn't believe that she was lucky, or that good things happened to someone 'like her', so she never put herself in the rooms or situations where anything exciting or extraordinary could ever actually happen.

She accepted, at an identity level that she wasn't the kind of person who was ever meant to be rich, so she acted with a poor money mindset, and self-sabotaged any attempts to ever create anything for herself. She also attracted low frequency people and situations, like unexpected bills, would continually loose her purse and would always have one financial drama after another. Her external reality was quite literally a reflection of her internal belief system of what she was worthy and capable of receiving.

There once was a study held in a research centre. The test subjects were either people who considered themselves to be lucky, or unlucky. They thought the test was related to a questionnaire that they were asked to complete. The actual test was that money was left outside of the test centre, on the floor. The test subjects were sent to lunch as part of the experiment. The people who considered themselves to be lucky, naturally found the money on the floor and the ones that considered themselves to be unlucky, walked right past it.

Creating radical awareness around how patterns and cycles show up for you, is the first step in reprogramming your internal beliefs system to one that serves you more.

4 – The Law of Attraction

This law is the relationship between your thoughts and how they create your reality. Your thoughts create vibrations, and that frequency attracts things with the same frequency. The guiding principle is that essentially that like energy attracts like energy. In the same way as The Law of Vibration, you attract what you are a match to.

This accounts for all things in the Universe, your thoughts, feelings, things. The Law of Attraction is always in motion, whether you are consciously aware of it or not.

You are the creator of your reality. The bitter pill that most struggle to swallow, is the awareness that they are creating their reality, the good, the bad and the ugly. Often people will fall into 'victim' mode, where they think that life is happening *to* them, instead of *from* them.

The good news is, when you know better, you can do better. Me really accepting the realisation that, because I had a deep routed feeling of unworthiness, when it came to money (because of my conditioning from others and my own past experiences), I was drawing low vibe people who would use me, was a real turning point in changing the game entirely.

I once googled contact details for local Sharman healers, because I believed that I was cursed, due to the bad luck I had experienced my whole life. I felt so utterly incapable of changing my life for the better, and for good, that I believed that a healer could help me instead.

I didn't realise that I had fallen into the same self-sabotaging belief system that my Mum had suffered from, because I had tried so hard to be so different from her. My life was completely different from hers, and my upbringing, but the same cycle of extreme highs, followed by huge lows, was undeniable.

I felt utterly powerless, until I read The Secret and realised that I was the one that had created my own 'upper limit', of happiness and success, that I felt comfortable with, and all the bad things that happened afterwards, were being manifested by me. This was a gamechanger in reclaiming my power.

Have you ever met people that are just seemingly super lucky, and good things always happen to them? In my experience the people that I had encountered were also narcissistic, and it always felt even more of an injustice. I realised after reading *The Secret* that a Narcissist has an inflated sense of ego, i.e., they think they are a big deal, and they expect good things to happen to them, because they are clearly better than the rest of us mere mortals. Thanks to the Law of Attraction, because they have this deep routed sense of importance and expectation, good things are attracted to them like a moth to a flame, whether it is fair or not. The good thing is, you can reclaim your power at any time, when you *decide* that your life gets to be better.

5 – The Law of Inspired Action

There is a common misconception when people talk about how to 'manifest' your best life, is that all you need to do, is stay positive and think good thoughts. In fact, the manifestation process, is a co-creative dialogue between you and the Universe.

To achieve your goals, you must also be open to receiving the inspired actions needed to get there. I call these 'downloads' and I often get them when I am in the shower, driving, or otherwise minding my own business.

Maybe you have had the same experience? These inspirational hits are the Universe's way of communicating with you, and giving you the steps, you need to take, to call in the thing that you want. I have learned not to second guess these ideas and move quickly when they come through.

They have taken my business in completely new and exciting directions, that I never could have logically planned for, and what keeps me obsessed with what I do. There is always another level that I can achieve. It's one thing to believe that what you want is possible, it's another to MOVE and take the action necessary to get it.

I often get asked 'How do you know the difference between action and *inspired action?*'. For me it's simple, Action feels like busy work, and can sometimes come with a lot of a fear or self-doubt. I will often see women in business chronically busy in their businesses, because they are worried that no-one else will care or do as good a job, because they think if they throw enough spaghetti at the wall, something will stick, or because being super busy makes them feel in control, or worthy of any success that is created.

They need to feel like they've 'earned it', to receive the monetary wins that come.

Inspired action feels completely different. It feels like a pull and a knowing, that whatever you do is going to equal a win, one way or another. The energy of that idea is infectious, and you're only job is not to overcomplicate the process or sit on it for too long.

Elizabeth Gilbert states in her book *'Big Magic'*, that inspiration and ideas are always trying to get our attention, but if we are too busy or consumed by our own lives, we can miss out on it entirely as an idea needs to be manifested, and if you ignore it, it will simply move on to someone else. This gave me chills when I read it, as I realised, I often had great ideas but allowed others to talk me out of them, because I believed everyone else knew better than me.

Who knows what incredible, innovative, and original ideas could have passed me by over the years before I found my own voice and allowed myself to fully step into my power?

Even writing this book, as much as I had a framework and a thought process of what I wanted to cover when I started, this book has taken many unexpected turns, plot twists and ventured down many rabbit holes. I believe the words that eventually have found their way onto these pages, are here because someone needed to hear them.

Maybe that's you?

As you reflect on this law, my invitation to you is to consider where you may potentially be blocking your flow of inspired action, making quick decisions and making moves in your business, because you are allowing logic, fear and perfectionism to make you second guess yourself?

6 – The Law of Perpetual Transmutation of Energy

This law states that everything is energy, and that the energy is constantly evolving from thought into matter or fluctuating its frequency. Our thoughts vibrate at a certain frequency, and whatever is a match for that frequency, is what is attracted to us. The challenge is that studies from the National Science Foundation show that we have up to 60,000 thoughts a day, and that 95% of those thoughts will be the same as the day before, and 80% of those thoughts will be negative.

We recycle thoughts as an energy saving process, this is why we form habits. Our brain wants to prioritise that all our energy stores are directed to pumping our blood, keeping our organs doing their thing, and keeping us alive. The more that it can automate or recycle our thoughts, the less energy it needs to send towards creating new ones.

We also have an inbuilt negativity bias, as a default mode, that means we are more likely to see the negative in any situation, as a way of keeping ourselves safe from negative outcomes. It's another of the brain's way of keeping us safe. The problem with this is that low vibe thoughts can be addictive, as we replay negative situations, as a way of trying to make sense of them.

Our brain is solutions focussed, the more it can determine either what went wrong, or who was to blame in any situation, the more you can make sense of it. When I had lost money or things didn't work out as I had hoped in the past, I had made sense of what happened, by DECIDING that it was because I wasn't good enough. I believed that I didn't have the same chance of success as everyone else because of my turbulent childhood.

I would therefore always feel like I was on the back foot and essentially took myself out of the game before I had even started. Energetically, my thoughts were at such a low frequency, believing that life would always be against me, and that I was powerless to change my situation, which had been reflected to me in my reality time and time again, that all I was attracting were situations that confirmed this.

To attract better opportunities and better outcomes, I had to create better thoughts. Ones that served me and raised my energy levels, ones that fired me up and got me motivated to go out and take the inspired actions needed, to achieve my goals.

I needed to reframe past bad experiences, like when my house was repossessed when I was a teenager, and extract the lessons and blessings from those situations, so that instead of providing evidence that bad things always happen to me, it reminded me how resourceful, strong and capable I am instead. It also reminded me that the Universe has a plan for each of us, that is bigger than we could even imagine, and that every setback sets us up for the ultimate comeback.

Journal Prompts:

What past experiences with money, or otherwise, are you still allowing to have power over you, and lower your vibrational frequency?

How can you reframe, make peace or extract the lessons from those situations, so that you feel more positive about them, and stop them from lowering your vibrations?

Equally, have you ever felt really excited about something, and told that idea to someone else, who has literally sucked all the vibrancy, life and energy out of that idea, with their own pessimistic view?

I call these people 'Energy Vampires' as they literally suck the life out of you, when you are around them. It's a tough one because usually these are the people that mean well, by spreading their cautionary tales of woe, all over you, to keep you safe. I encountered lots of these people when I was pregnant with my first child, I suddenly became magnetic to anyone with a traumatic labour stories, and felt compelled to share it with me.

Do you have anyone like that in your life right now?

How can you protect your energy, so that their low vibe doesn't infect your own, and bring you down to their level?

7 – The Law of Cause and Effect

This law states that for every cause there is an effect. For every thought that we have, there is an outcome reflected back to us in our reality. Every outcome is a reflection of a decision or action that you have taken. Everything that you put out into the world, has a ripple effect (like karma), that will come back to you at some point or another. If you put intentions and thoughts filled with anger and resentment, that energy will come back to you.

You might feel right now that life is happening to you, but this law confirms that life is happening from you instead. Great news when you realise the absolute powerhouse that you are, and decide to put that energy, intention and confidence into achieving those big, audacious goals that you secretly hold in your heart.

Often when I start working with clients, they have an inner knowing that they are meant for greatness, but they are embarrassed of those big desires and missions. Society has taught us to be 'good girls' who are nice, humble, don't take up too much space, don't want too much for ourselves and aren't too confident or outspoken.

My work as a mentor, is to unpick those beliefs and reprogram them into more serving ones, so my they can step into the Queen that they were always meant to be.

Wealth is your birthright, and the world needs you to shine at your brightest level, so you can impact change at the highest level too. No-one wins when you play small or dim your light for others. I always say, if your goals don't excite, expand, or embarrass you, you aren't thinking big enough!

So, if your thoughts have consequences, and are every day tipping the scale, and moving you either towards or away from your goals, how are your current thoughts serving you?

Learning this law was so comforting for me, as I realised bad things weren't happening to me, as random acts of cruelty from The Universe, but were happening as an opportunity to shine a light on the parts of me that still needing healing.

I was thinking, behaving, and acting from the mindset of a traumatised 7-year-old, who still felt the sting of abandonment from her family. As a result, I had also abandoned myself, and my right to be worthy of success and happiness, just because I was.

8 – The Law of Compensation

This is one of my favourite laws and essentially encompasses the mantra – 'you reap what you sow', every good deed is adding up in your favour, and you will at some point be compensated for it.

Equally, you must give before you expect something in return. I often see this as a challenge when working with clients in their relationships with partners. They complain that they expect their partners to just 'know' that they want them to buy them flowers or do something nice unexpectedly, and yet when I ask them how often they do that for their partners, I am usually met with never.

If you aren't prepared to go first, and show your partner how you want to be treated, how can they respond, simply by knowing?

In your business, this implies that to be a leader in your industry, who has a huge following on social media and bank of clients ready to buy your offers, you must first be a woman worthy of being followed.

This looks like:

- Showing up and adding value to your audience online before asking for a sale (Buy a girl a drink first)
- Being a woman of integrity and a walking, talking embodiment of your work, before asking your clients to follow your advice.
- Cultivating meaningful relationships with your clients and potential clients, and not focussing solely on the sale, whether they buy or not, that intention and act of service, will come back to you in a positive way, one way or another.
- Committing to mastering your craft, and getting results for your clients, before expecting people to invest in you
- I always loved the book '*The Thank You Economy* by multi-millionaire and Business Entrepreneur, Gary Vaynerchuk, who embodies the same values. He says "*It's not the number of followers you have or "likes" you get, it's the strength of your bond with your followers that indicates how much anyone cares about what you have to say. In this game, the one with the most real relationships wins.*".

9 – The Law of Relativity

This law suggests that our happiness can be skewed by comparing it to other's success. It states that everything can only be made real, by its relationship to something else. When we can instead, approach every challenge or curveball from a neutral position, and see it as an opportunity for personal growth, it no longer has the power to affect us negatively.

We have removed the emotional charge. What once used to trigger us into a negative spiral, i.e., when you see others on social media seemingly smashing it in life, when you are struggling, you can now see that it just an opportunity to see the success that is available to you too. If they can do it, you can do it too.

I always say to my clients, when they are having a tough time in their business, when nothing feels like it's working, that this moment is actually a blessing.

If Oprah's story to fame was less of a hero's journey, and more like easy street, would she be the unstoppable powerhouse she is Today? Would you have the same level of resilience, creativity, resourcefulness, and inner fortitude? Hell No?

Equally, would we be as endeared to her, if everything she had achieved in her career, had been handed to her on a plate? Probably not!

Whenever times were tough, on my journey to financial empowerment, as awful and hard and traumatic as it felt at the time, the person who emerged on the other side of the adversity always had the ability to shock, inspire and love myself a little more deeply.

After a lifetime of feeling shame, embarrassment, and unworthiness, because of my turbulent childhood and lack of belonging, I reclaimed my power by having the word 'Damaged' tattooed on my wrist. This for me, was a moment.

It was me redefining what that word meant, and how it felt to be associated as someone who was 'damaged'. The actual truth is, trauma is relative to the person, what feels like a big deal to us, without a point of reference that exceeds that pain, might be small fry to someone else. I used to struggle when trying to connect with new friends at high school when they would be so consumed by boy drama, and looking nice, when I was worried about how I could finish school, if my then family member kicked me out (which happened), as, after already repeating my final year due to a huge geographical move, I had officially run out of options.
I ached to have such normal and basic problems, I always felt the weight of the absolute world crashing down on me, while also trying to support my Mum and siblings who I felt that I had left behind. I realised however, that to those girls, the weight of the world was also crashing down on them too.

Their 'trauma' was relative to what they had experienced in life up until that point, and my lack of empathy, was unfair, because I was trying to invalidate their pain, because I was frustrated at how my life continued to play out. I would feel guilty, about having these thoughts of frustration, because I so desperately wanted to be a 'good person', as if someone, somewhere was taking score and deciding, that when I was a good enough person, the cards for me would be re-dealt and things would suddenly get better.

 The reality is, we are all damaged in our own way, and that adversity is what makes us the incredible, layered, badass women we are Today.

Choosing to reframe our pain, and reclaim our power, is the first step in *becoming* the most empowered version of us.

I always say, if someone is having a tough time in business right now, and they feel like they have lost all hope, that I am excited for them. The person who emerges on the other side of that challenge, will have been tested and will emerge with a whole new set of skills, resourcefulness, creativity, innovation and zero fucks out of the bag, that they can then use as a point of reference, in every other part of their life, as a continual reminder of who the F they are, and what magic they can achieve when their back is against the wall.

Reframing failure, and embracing it, as a means of feedback and expansion, is the number one thing that built my entrepreneurial toolkit and has cultivated my unstoppable mindset in business. As a result, it has also healed parts of myself personally, that I was previously ashamed or felt guilty about.

I can now see these as triumphs, rather than failures and I no longer see the word 'damaged' (which was once used by a narcissistic ex-boyfriend as an insult, and a way to hurt me), as a bad thing. I have reclaimed the very definition of the word, as a badge of honour instead.

10 – The Law of Polarity

This law states that everything has an opposite, and that this duality is needed to create balance in our Universe. If our life was continually good, would it feel so good without the contrast of bad periods too? Would we be able to grow and expand and reach our fullest expression and potential in this lifetime, if everything was always one continual Instagram highlight reel? Probably not!

We need the balance of the light and the dark, the good and the bad, to really appreciate them both. I truly believe that the financial losses that I have experienced in life have given me such a deeper appreciation for the relationship that I have with money now. It's also given me perspective that money alone will not make you happy, controversial I know, as a Money Mindset Mentor. It's the abundance in ALL areas of life, that truly equal happiness and success.

Equally in yourself, you must embrace the dark and light. If there are personality traits or desires that don't fit the acceptable standards of society, that's ok. You are here to learn to love and embrace both parts and see the opportunities for personal growth.

I'm not Snow White, who walks around as an angel on earth 24/7, sometimes I lose my shizzle with my kids, I judge, I worry, I have desires that aren't all about the greater good of the collective (sometimes a woman just wants something boujee AF, and that's ok!) I speak before thinking but rather than making myself bad or wrong, I love myself regardless.

I know my heart; I'm a good person and I am a HUMAN! Perfection does not exist; I am sure Mother Teresa still had a guilty pleasure at times. Life is going to ebb and flow, like the tides of the sea, there will be a season where things feel harder than easier and that's ok! It's exactly as it is meant to be.

In money terms, there will be times in your business where it just gets better and better, it's why I love to focus on building Monthly Reoccurring Revenue, and encouraging my clients to do the same, rather than creating high cash months. It isn't because I don't believe that there will always be more clients and more opportunities to make money, but because there will inevitably be times where you don't want to be ON or IN your business, so the more stability and safety you have in your monthly income, the better equipped you will be to work with those times. It's Universal law.

I have seen many a woman come unstuck in business, when they had a good run, overcommitted to high expenses, that they then couldn't sustain when the law of polarity kicked in, and their business took a temporary dip.

This downturn sent them running back to the perceived safety of corporate, saw them racking up debts and or internalising their dip as a moment of failure, and confirmation that they are not good enough.

11 – The Law of Rhythm

We are naturally cyclical beings. The moon's cycles, our menstrual cycles, the seasons of the weather, the ebb and flow of the tides, everything works in rhythms and cycles. It blows my mind then, as women, why we put so much pressure to be on ourselves to build our businesses in the same way as a man.

This looks like working 5-7 days a week, every week, and being constantly ON and IN our business. When I first started out in business, and had bought my Barber Shop, it was a 7 day a week commitment. The shop was open from 8am to 8pm and I put myself under so much pressure to be there as much as I could, even though I had 3 young children, even when I was sick, and only had 1 days Maternity leave when I gave birth with my fourth baby.

Everything I did was either from a place of expectation or fear. Expectation came from being part of the 'Boss Babe' era, where it was normalised to hustle and grind your way to success and being the hardest working person in the room, to prove that you had what it took to be successful.

I also had a lot of fear around the financial stakes of my success. I was a single parent, who was officially unemployable, who had gone all in on her business and had no plan B or anyone who could (or would) help me, if things went wrong. I felt the weight of my decision to buy my business at every level, topped off with a huge amount of mum guilt for all the lost weekends, and holidays, as I tried to do ALL the things. I was scared that people would steal from me or sabotage my business (which they did and tried to do), if I wasn't there all the time.

I was afraid to enjoy my success fully in case the Universe thought that I was too full of myself and decided to punish me as a result. I was afraid of everything, and I had very little confidence in myself to be ok, whatever came next.

I didn't believe that me taking time off, would mean that my energy could be restored, and I would come back stronger and better than before. I also didn't want to say no to people and opportunities, in case I was seen as rude, ungrateful or in case more opportunities wouldn't follow if I missed out on this one thing. This is a common, toxic trait of burnt-out women in business.

We are so busy sucking it up, being consistent, pushing through it, and trying to stay focussed, that we are missing the point of being a business owner at all. Your business gets to work around you, not the other way around. It's your party, and you get to do what you want to.

And then, for me and like so many others, COVID happened, and the world stood still. For the first time in my whole life, I had permission to stop chasing my tail, doing all the things, and working myself to the bone. I had a moment to reflect, take stock and decide, with intention what my next steps were going to be. I am so grateful for that time, for that reason.

When I emerged from the other side of lockdown, I had more clarity and conviction that my current business model at that time did not serve me, and I leaned all the way into scaling my coaching business, that had been ticking along at that point. I was so excited to follow my soul's purpose, be of higher service and equally enjoy the flexibility that I craved. I made sure, that I then did not create another job, with 24/7 commitments, by intentionally planning my weeks and automating my business, so that I didn't need to be on, all the time.

Now, I get to harness my bursts of energy in creative ways and pull back in times when I need to put my energy elsewhere, either because I need a rest or because there are other things in my life that feel like a priority at that moment. My business has grown strength to strength ever since. This is why I support my clients to grow and scale their businesses in SUSTAINABLE, and STACKABLE ways, that means they get to have abundance in all areas of life, which to me is the real measure of success.

Where can you pay more attention to your natural energy cycles, and harness that energy in life and your business?

How can you build more flexibility, or work on the paradigms that tell you that you can't, so that you can rest and retreat when you need to, rather than pushing through these moments instead.

How can you be more supported, either by a team, automations, strategy, passive income or by asking, so that when you stop, your business (and your money-making potential) doesn't have to stop too.

12 – The Law of Gender

The balance of the divine masculine and feminine energy, exists in all of us. We need to have both, to create and produce in nature.

Whilst society favours masculine energy, that is focussed on DOING, rather than BEING, we need both. As women, we often pride ourselves on how much we can do and get done, how many plates we can spin, and how much shizzle we can handle. When we prioritise this push energy and focus, trying to make things happen, we miss a huge opportunity, to embrace our feminine energy as well.

I believe that there is a huge lack of originality and innovation in the online space right now, and it's becoming a very uninspiring place to be. Women are too busy looking around at others, to give them the answers as to how they can create success, and make money, rather than looking within. Tony Robins famously said *'success leave clues'*, and this has been misinterpreted to mean that if this strategy created success for someone else, then I must follow their system religiously to be successful myself.

This then leads to feelings of unworthiness, when you don't get the same results, believing you have done something wrong.

I once had a client Chloe who came to me with this very challenge. She had invested heavily into several coaching programs, that all taught a different way of launching her offers. All were totally out of alignment with her natural zone of genius (which was building intimate relationships with her clients) or energy levels, and she was stuck live launching her offers feeling like she needed to 'put on a show' for people to allow her to help them.

When she didn't get the crazy '£100k' launches that the coaching industry loves to promote, she felt like a failure, and was triggered by childhood trauma and feelings of not being worthy.

Investing in these programs had not empowered her to go out and create success at a higher level, they had instead put her on a negative downward spiral, causing her to shrink instead of expanding. When we began working together, there was a lot of hurt and feelings of rejection that we needed to heal and neutralise, before we could even get to the strategy part, as to how to showcase her gifts and make it easy for people to invest with her.

Instead of putting the pressure on one launch, as if she only had one shot of success, what felt more sustainable and aligned was an evergreen sales model.

This meant that people could invest in her offers at any time, and that her whole personal brand and business outputs also consistently uplevelled each month by creating better quality content, and more intentional customer journeys, plus free or low-ticket masterclasses that continued to showcase her talents.

We also leant into her superpower – her relationship building ability, by offering a high-ticket program, that she didn't rely on a high volume of sales, so that she could intentionally cherry pick the clients and past clients that she thought would be perfect for this offer.

It was a win, win as she has consistently built her monthly reoccurring revenue (the holy grail of female business owners), uplevelled her personal brand and expert status, through quality content, so clients now track her down, rather than her feeling like she was speaking to a void, and having to convince people to work with her. The whole journey was so fulfilling for me as a Mentor, to be part of, as she blossomed into an absolute badass who learned to stop looking outside of herself for answers, and instead look within, so that she could create sustainable success on her own terms.

To be clear, we need a balance of masculine energy to fully express our potential, too much of one or the other would see us either having a great vision of what we want to achieve, but doing absolutely nothing about it, or trying to force an outcome by continually being in push energy instead. All things in the Universe have a balance of both:

Divine Masculine energy is focussed on action and doing, rather than being. It's connected to the warrior in each of us and symbolises strength, conviction, determination, and confidence. It embodies generosity, service and giving energy to others. We need our masculine energy to stay accountable to our goals, be decisive, move forwards and get shizzle done.

Feminine Energy is all about being, rather than doing, and connecting to your own divine source of inspiration, resourcefulness, and creativity. It represents collaboration and receiving support from others. It's ironic as a woman that we often end up stuck in our masculine energy, giving our time to everyone else, and never asking for support ourselves. I believe there is a lack of innovation in the online space, because women are not connecting to their divine feminine energy enough for a source of inspiration and guidance, because society has conditioned us to be chronically busy, second guess ourselves and fit in with the status quo, like everyone else. If we could see feminine energy as the incredible gift that it is, the world would be a much more exciting place!

Here's the thing, every successful entrepreneur needs to have a balance of the two energies, to fully optimise their businesses. Even successful male entrepreneurs like Sir Richard Branson, Simon Cowell and Jeff Bezos would have to be in touch with their feminine energy to be able to forge meaningful relationship with business partners and clients, find innovative and creative solutions to problems and bring innovative and fresh ideas to their markets.

Take a moment to reflect on where you may be favouring one energy type for another, which could be costing you money and fulfilment in the long run?

So why do you need to know about all these spiritual principals, to have more money, inside and outside of your business?

For me, it helped me to redefine my relationship with money, and give it the context it needed. For years, I had put 'money' on a pedestal, believing it was the answer to all my problems. The reality is, because I hadn't worked on my internal beliefs, it didn't matter how much money I made, it would always find somewhere else to go and I would end up back at zero.

Learning the principals of the 12 spiritual laws, reminded me that money is just energy. It's an exchange of value and nothing more than that. It didn't have morals or beliefs, it wouldn't go to whoever was 'worthy' or good enough, it would flow to whoever gave it the least resistance.

It would then stay wherever it was desired, nurtured and appreciated. It was just the same as any other relationship in your life, that needed to be nurtured, and it was one that could evolve and strengthen over time.

Giving it so much power, as a separate entity outside of yourself, that would only flow to you if you meet some arbitrary measure of being 'good enough', is only keeping you further away from receiving it.

Instead, understanding that money is just energy, and that as we are all connected (as per the Law of Divine Oneness), reminded me that I had just the same chance as anyone else, regardless of my past experiences of making money, and living a more abundant life.

This was a gamechanger for me and a turning point, in reclaiming my own personal power, and the hold that 'money' had over me. It no longer felt like this magical unicorn, that I needed to be perfect to receive.

How has learning these spiritual laws, changed your understanding of how money works, and how you tap into the frequency of wealth, to attract more in to your life?

STRATEGY
- MONEY MAKING

CHAPTER 8

Financially Optimising Your Business

"God did not fuck up when he made you or when he gave you your desire" – Amanda Frances

In business communities, I am often known as The Queen of Leverage, thanks to my innate ability to get the most bang for my buck, when it comes to using my time efficiently to get the best results, financially as I have over 27 revenue streams, and energetically as I only have 2 days childcare a week. I am all about the work smarter, not harder philosophy.

This comes down to my Human Design, which is a Manifesting Generator, and a common profile amongst multi-passionate entrepreneurs. I also have undeniable symptoms of ADHD (although I haven't been tested because I don't need a label), and I learned a long time ago, that I was never going to be a woman that does things like everyone else.

If you are familiar with Human Design (HD), you will know that a Manifesting Generator (MG), is meant to be led by their passions, and ensure that they don't get too boxed in, or tied down creatively. I often use HD as a way to create truly aligned sales and marketing strategies for my clients, but due to the context of this book, I won't be going into too much detail about that approach here.

Perhaps there will be another book on this, send me a message on Instagram @thefemalepreneurcoach if you would like to learn more about this fascinating approach.

You can also visit my blog for more resources on all things money, mindset, business, and spiritual practices www.thefemalepreneurcoach.co.uk/blog.

Human Design is a combination of ancient energy systems, such as Astrology, the Chinese I Ching, the Kaballah, Tree of Life, the Hindu Chakra and scientific principles of Neuroscience, Biochemistry & Quantum Mechanics. It is essentially a blueprint of who your 'best self' is meant to be at a soul level, so that you can operate, and create success in the most aligned way to you and your energy type.

Whether you are aware of your HD profile or not, playing to your natural strengths and talents, to market and deliver your business is always going to lead to sustainable and stackable success.

If you are reading this book, I am assuming that you are either already a woman in business, or an aspiring one. In this chapter, I will share with you the basic principles of earning a great income online, in your purpose-driven business.

If you don't yet have a business, and aren't sure where to start, I would love to invite you to join me inside any of my business building programs, where I can help you to discover your zone of genius, your passion, and how you can apply those to growing a soulful business. Your gifts have value, and you deserve to be compensated for sharing them in hundreds of ways that make other's lives better. As Entrepreneurs we are ultimately solution providers, and you sharing your gifts is making someone else's lives better. What a beautiful thing!.

Whichever route you take, you have value to share with the world, and transferrable skills that could shortcut someone else's journey. You only need to be two steps ahead of someone else, to add value to that person. Whether those two steps are in making the perfect birthday cake, healing past trauma, or writing a highly converting sales page, it all counts, and it can all be monetised in many different ways.

Sales Mindset

Hopefully by this point in the book, you have already started to understand that money is an exchange of energy, and getting paid well for your work, is a win for everyone. The reason I really need to hammer in this point, is because I have worked with so many incredible women over the years, that have amazing gifts to share with the world, but the thought of putting themselves out there stops them in their tracks.

This causes them to:

- Resist making invitations to their prospective clients to work with them, preferring to 'friend zone' their leads instead, so as not to seem too 'salesy'. This goes on forever, until it would then become awkward to suddenly bring up your offers, kind of like when someone calls you by the wrong name, but it goes on too long it would be weird to correct them.

- Focus on marketing low-ticket offers, thinking that the cheaper the price-point, the easier it will be to sell. The reality, its actually the reverse. Lower ticket prices can attract clients who are more fearful around spending, and want everything including the kitchen sink thrown in, to reconcile the purchase for themselves. It's easier to sell high-ticket offers, as high-ticket clients tend to be more self-led and know already what they want. If you can deliver on their desires, its already a hell yes from them.

- At the other end of the spectrum, they can also focus on selling their high-ticket 1:1 offers only, as the income is more meaningful, but don't have a smart offer suite in place, so they end up leaving money on the table when they don't have a down-sell in place, for prospective clients who can't afford their 1:1 price. They can also become overbooked and exhausted, when they don't have a scalable offer to sell, that leverages their time and energy.

- Overdeliver on their offers, to the point of unsustainability as they become overly responsible for their clients' results, too accessible, with no boundaries in place, and throw in the aforementioned kitchen sink, which leaves them with 100 add on elements to deliver. Build every offer with the view that you are going to sell hundreds, if not thousands of your offers. I once had a client who offered afternoon tea with her, as a bonus to signing up. She had already energetically cock-blocked her money goal, as she could not physically have afternoon tea with all the people who would need to sign up to hit it. Unless she wanted to create another full time, job and was being paid commission by the scones company.

- Are in a continual feast and famine cycle where they go all in on their sales strategy, possibly through live launching, then get bogged down with the delivery needed for their new clients. This causes them to drop the ball, until they realise, they are about to offboard their clients, and have no new leads in site, so must frantically panic-post on socials to try and claw in some new clients, just to pay their bills.

- Over invest, or under invest in their business, which stunts its growth, scalability, and fun!!

- Tell themselves lies about what their potential clients will and won't pay, by looking to others in their industries (who are also probably dealing with their own money shizzle) to set the average prices and go with those.

- Leave money on the table, and obvious opportunities to increase sales, because they want to be a good person and not focus too much on the money. God forbid you might want to make the world a better place, AND feed your kids in the process, what a terrible person you must be. The audacity!!

- Listen to internet marketing gurus, who tell them that they can make £100k in their pants, by doing absolutely no work, and when they can't replicate that person's success (*because they failed to mention they had an ad spend that equalled a deposit on a house, and a team of 20 in the background*) they are left feeling like absolute failures, and running back to corporate.

- Resist selling often enough, or intentionally enough, to give them the success that they deserve. If you want to make money daily in your business, with sales on repeat, you need to give people the opportunity to benefit from your services daily too.

Your desired experience around money in your business, needs to be a match your input. You can't show up once a week to talk about your offers and expect to make it rain.

Plus, contrary to popular belief, people are not actually obsessed with you. They are busy and could easily miss that one time offer post, in a sea of newsfeed updates. Being consistent with your sales offers, builds trust, and increases the likelihood that the right people will see what you have to offer, at the right time and MOVE.

- Lack confidence or conviction in what they are selling, so they never make any meaningful number of sales, or reach their full income or impact potential.

Remember we are all unconsciously looking for our tribal leader, who knows more than we do, to show us the way. If you aren't confident about the results you can create for your clients, they will feel that energetically, and won't feel compelled to buy now.

People buy certainty, so if you don't believe that everyone would be an absolute idiot if they didn't work with you, then you are going to have a problem with converting your clients.

Let's normalise owning the shizzle out of our gifts. You're a big deal, own it, and watch your conversions soar. Even if you don't have scroll-stopping, OMFG results YET, you know the heart, passion and integrity, you will bring to the table, to ensure your clients get what they want. Stop keeping all that incredibleness inside you, the best kept secret in your industry.

Journal Prompts:

What experience would you like to create around money and sales in your business?

Does your input match your desired output?

What are the beliefs that you have around money and pricing in your business, that could be keeping you stuck right now?

What part of you does not want to achieve your next level of visibility and success in business?

All these things, feel like a crime against nature, and are the reason that I am such a fierce champion of other women in business, and feel so passionately about supporting them to step into their most financially empowered self.

As much as internet marketing guru's love to complicate the process of sales, it's actually very simple. It's an exchange of value and nothing more or less than that. I hate it when I hear people talk about 'charging your worth', because ultimately you are priceless baby girl, and no one could ever afford you!

Separating your self-worth from the financial exchanges in your business, is a great first step towards reclaiming your power from money.

As entrepreneurs and business owners, we are solution providers, people need what we have, and it would be rude not to share it. I was once at a boujee retreat in LA and a fabulous woman I met there, Jeanette Carbajal (@thespiritualbusinesshealer) said something that has stuck with me ever since *'The world will be healed by Entrepreneurs'*.. chills! When I really thought about that statement, it activated me more than ever, to want to get out and share my business with as many women as possible.

Think about her statement for a moment. Every person you serve, whether you are selling self-development or self-care, you make someone's life a little better, with the solutions that you provide. You're a bit of a badass, and we just need more people to know that.

As simple as sales are, you still need to have a few things in place, to maximise your opportunity to serve at the highest level. Selling is serving, after all.

1 – An Irresistible Offer for Your Ideal Client

Yes - ideal client, not the person that you think will actually pay for your service or product. In business, it's your party and you get to choose who you work with, so you might as well make sure it is someone that you cannot wait to jump on a call with or talk about your incredible solution to their problem.

With any offer that you create, what is the desire or outcome that the clients want from that thing?

How can you think big picture when you are marketing your offers?

How can you really lean in and understand how this will positively affect them, at every level?

How bold can you make the promise, if your ideal client were to lean in, follow all the steps and fully leverage your expertise?

How would your offer literally change their life?

I once had a client who had a bespoke fashion brand. She wanted to set up a subscription option for her clients, where they would send her their measurements and she would send a monthly subscription box filled with beautifully tailored fashion items. She came to me when she had first created her sales page but had yet to get any interest or orders in her new venture.

For me, it was super clear what had gone wrong. She hadn't got into the mindset of her ideal client and really thought about the outcome of her work. Upon digging deeper, I connected the dots with her to move from a low converting sales page with little to no interest from her current audience to an actual movement in female empowerment, with national press coverage.

The thing is, yes, her ideal client wanted nice clothes but for them, the desire went so much deeper. They wanted to feel sexy and confident. They didn't want to conform to societies' expectations of what a size 12 should look like, they didn't want to have to wear ill-fitting clothes that sapped them of their confidence and made them feel shameful of their curves. They wanted to be seen and heard on their own terms.

They wanted to feel fabulous and accepted, exactly as they were. This feeling would ripple out into their home life, social life and work and make them feel powerful, confident, and unstoppable.

Once we had worked together to update the sales page, we also added a social media campaign to add excitement around the relaunch, and a Facebook group community was built around prospective leads to add value and build community. When we relaunched the offer, we had a fabulous online party with the members of the Facebook community, filled with prospective clients and the launch was a huge hit. Add some national press coverage, thanks to the refined marketing campaign and it was a sold-out launch!

This is just one example of where my client had got 'lost' in her business, and in the delivery of her offers. She couldn't pick herself up and look at what she was selling, and what the benefits of that would be for her clients.

This meant she was massively underselling the transformation and the desire of her subscription. Taking a moment to think bigger, allowed us to completely refocus her launch and brought in an incredible community of passionate, like-minded loyal clients, that made her delivery so much more fun too.

2 – A Sustainable Business Model

I believe the reasons that female entrepreneur has the highest startup and close rate in business, is because they are building businesses that put them in a continual state of conflict. This means they have one foot on the gas, and one foot on the break, and ultimately become their own block to success.

This looks like:

- Running their business in a way that requires them to be on 24/7, essentially in the same way that a man would run it. Here's the thing, as women we are cyclical beings and are not meant to be on 'go mode' all day, all night. Our businesses should be built with the flexibility to ebb and flow, like the tides, peaks and troughs of our energy levels, cycles of the moon and in line with our menstrual cycles.

This is where smart automations, funnels, teams and strategic sales and marketing plans can be created to allow your business to run without you, so when you stop, your income doesn't have to stop too.

- Trying to do things that they have no business doing, so they end up doing it badly and it becomes a completely pointless exercise.

When I bought my first business, a Barber shop, my first instinct was not to learn how to cut hair, so I could save the wage of a Barber. To the male population of my local town – YOU ARE WELCOME! I dread to think the madness that could have ensued. I am blessed with super straight hair, but even I bought a set of hair straighteners, after being dazzled by the aesthetically pleasing AF advertising campaigns of GHDs. Not only was my hair not any straighter, glossier, or shinier, when I first used them, but I actually ended up ironing a crease into the top of my hair, that was so eye-twitching I had to rewash my hair to get rid of it. I immediately gave my straighteners away as a result. Needless to say, I have no natural talent that relates to hair.

In the book 'The Big Leap' by Gay Hendricks, he encourages us to work within our 'Zone of Genius', and do the things that we do well, rather than waste unnecessary time and energy trying to compensate for the things that we don't. He uses four zones to represent this point:

Zone of Incompetence – The things that you quite literally have no business in doing. You don't enjoy them, you aren't very good at them, and no amount of perseverance or personal development will change that.

For me they include Cooking for pleasure (yawn), cleaning my bathroom and doing repetitive tasks repeatedly. Thankfully I've found workarounds for each of these items, by cultivating a love of eating out in my 5 children, so we can still make mealtimes fun, I have a cleaner who gets so much satisfaction from cleaning the bathroom, and I automate, eliminate, or delegate repetitive tasks in my business.

What are those things for you?

Zone of Competence – Things you are ok at, and possibly even good at, but they don't light your soul on fire to complete them, and you have no interest in getting better at them. For me, in my business, these are things like editing videos, I can do them, but I have no desire to become a world class video editor, nor would I see that as a good use of my time. I would much rather outsource that to someone else who lives for it and is an expert in their field.

What are those things for you?

Zone of Excellence – Things you are naturally good at, even if you don't know why. For some reason, I have mastered the art, with 3 girls, of a French plait, at lightning speed thanks to years of practice with impatient, squirming toddlers. I also find tech, spreadsheets, funnels, and automations easy, whereas others can find these more challenging.

The Zone of Excellence is also known as the danger zone for this reason. As much as banging out a quick landing page or email nurture sequence satisfies my inner tech nerd, is it really the best use of my time, as a CEO of my business? This is where most women can stay stuck, because busy work, that feels easy, makes us feel in control, validated and we love to tell ourselves saves us money.

Often you might say things like 'I can do it quickly, so I might as well do it, to save myself some money', 'no one will do it as good as I will and I'll save some money', 'I don't mind doing it and it saves me money'.. notice the pattern? That money that you are 'saving' by not investing in a team or support, is probably costing you a lot more than you think in the long run, as you miss and sometimes actively avoid opportunities to make money, by getting bogged down in the minutia of running your business.

What are those things for you?

Zones of Genius – This is the sweet spot of doing the things that you naturally love and are really bloody good at. These are the things that see you in flow, where you lose time doing them, and would probably do them whether you were paid or not. They are probably the things that have always been part of your nature, and typically, if you are like me, the things you used to get distracted with when you were young, and therefore continually told off for.

For me, it was talking. I was always a chatty Cathy, who loved to collect connections with everyone I met, from kids at school, to old ladies I chatted with in ques at Tescos, to drunk girls abandoned by their boyfriends, hiding in nightclub toilets. I have always naturally been a great connector of people, and affiliate commissions have been a huge part of my business, as I have referred over six figures of business to other female-led businesses in just the last 12 months alone.

I also have a podcast and host transformational, boujee AF in-person events. I've also been known to throw a mean Halloween party, and one of the most festive people you will ever meet. All these things LIGHT ME UP, get me excited to literally catapult out of bed in the morning, and magnetise my ideal client, who love my high vibe energy.

When I work with my clients, these are the elements that we focus on adding to their business, so it feels as easy, fun and aligned as possible. This, to me is the key to longevity in business and really what it's all about. If you are ever unsure about whether you can monetise the gifts in your zone of genius and feel the pressure of trying to be 'realistic',

I once saw a woman on TV make six-figures from selling dead mice. I'm not joking. She literally dug up dead mice from her garden and shaped them into comical poses, using props such as Hoole hoops and roller skates and sold them online. I am energetically clapping for this woman, who realised there are always easier ways to make money and went for the one that felt the most fun to do. Hopefully, she is not a serial killer on the weekends.

What are the things in your zone of genius, and how can you add more of those to your business model?

- Low balling their results and their prices, so they have to hustle and juggle hundreds of clients, just to pay the bills, keeping them in a continual feast and famine cycle. At the other end of the spectrum, I also see women with the most entitled, unrealistic expectations of their income potential, because they saw someone else on the internet say they made £100k in their pants, without doing any work at all. When they don't get the same results, they end up deflated and running back to corporate, tail between their legs, adding another personal trauma to their belt notch. I'll talk more about pricing with integrity shortly.

- Delivering their services in a way that is not scalable or sustainable. For the women at back, that need the reminder, when it comes to business, it's your party and you can do what you want to. If you don't want to work evenings, don't. If you don't want to work with clients on a 1:1 basis, don't. If you don't want to nurture a Facebook community, don't.

You get to choose, and realising that, is one of the most empowering things that you can do as a CEO. For me, as a Mumma with 5 young children, I initially fell into the trap of needing to do all the things, to make life as easy for my clients, because I was scared, they wouldn't want to work with me otherwise.

This saw me working evenings, even though I am usually in bed by 9, and my home life with 5 different staggered bedtimes, was not set up to support it. I worked half-terms, and frantically tried to bribe my kids to be quiet or threaten to stuff them in cupboards, so I could get through my client calls. It wasn't until my 5-year-old (who I thought was asleep at the time), sensing I was distracted on a call, decided to give himself a very aggressive haircut, that I decided enough was enough, and that my business needed to work round me, and not the other way around.

A huge uplevelling in boundaries, intention, and focus ensued, and I ended up attracting the most incredible, self-led, unicorn clients who were happy to work round my schedule. Not only did they want to be on calls in the evening either, because they had partners, family, and a life to get on with, but they also respected my confidence and zero-fucks attitude, as it gave them permission to take the same approach with their own clients. Girl, stop being apologetic for having commitments or desires outside of your business, shed the corporate mindset and understand that your clients need you, more than you need them. You get to do it your way. Even if you just want to pop to a yoga class on a Tuesday, and would instead prefer to work evenings, you get to decide!

3 – A Stackable Offer Suite

When I opened my Barber shop, it was what we call in the industry, 'a £10 Barber Shop', which is essentially one that relies on high volumes of low-ticket customers to make ends meet. This means the customer service was terrible, the staff were absolutely shattered and the shop itself looked tired and battered. I did not want to continue this model, the thought of it exhausted me.

I instantly increased the price of an average haircut to £25, and uplevelled every aspect of the staff, environment, products, and customer experience to match the increase in expectations. I also gave clients reasons to come back again and again, through loyalty programs, and found additional ways to upsell them, to increase their Cost Per Head (CPH), by launching a men's grooming product range, that was featured in GQ magazine.

No one told me to do these things, but it made sense to me that more doesn't always equal more if I was burning through my staff, the shop, and clients. It was short term pleasure, for long term pain and I am not about that life.

Plus, I could see that this model was not sustainable, as if it rained or there were sports playing (aka economic downturns), the footfall of the Highstreet (and my income) fell dramatically. I've seen this trend play out in the online space, where women are encouraged to low ball themselves, and forget their transferrable skills, or previous experience, when first starting their business and be grateful for every client who will pay them.

I once had a client who wanted to grow her business as a Social Media Manager, so she could replace her corporate salary. She had been trained by another SM Manager, who had advised her to sell unsustainable £15 hashtag sets, as she was 'new to the industry and needed to do establish her client base'. I get this to a point, when I first started coaching, I was selling my business services for £350 for 6 weeks and was then puzzled why I had 8 clients sign up in one day, literally biting my hand off at the invitation.

Obviously, I had massively lowballed myself and negated my years of entrepreneurship, as I hadn't technically built a funnel before.

I'm sure you can imagine the nightmare 6 weeks that followed, as I built multiple funnels, sales, and marketing campaigns, launched offers and memberships, and juggled 8 very demanding clients who must have thought I was an idiot for chasing so little in exchange. For my client however, once I showed her the math of needing to sell hundreds of hashtag sets, to replace her salary, she finally got it.

I quickly established that she had lots of experience in growing an audience online, as she had built a very popular Mum Blog online, which is why she was interested in becoming a SM Manager in the first place. She already had an advantage over everyone else in her group coaching program, and yet she was hiding that talent and potential, because she was blindly following her mentor's advice.

Her mentor, who was boasting six figure launches, on her own socials, I suspect, did not get there by selling £15 hashtag sets. We decided very quickly to scrap her current offer suite and replace it for one that was more aligned to her skillset, didn't require all her personal energy to execute, and allowed her to increase her client's lifetime value and cost per head. Not only did we hit her income goal, with ease, in just a couple of weeks, we tripled it within the first month. Her business has gone from strength to strength ever since.

For me, a smart offer suite, or the way in which you deliver your services or products, needs to have the following levels or layers:

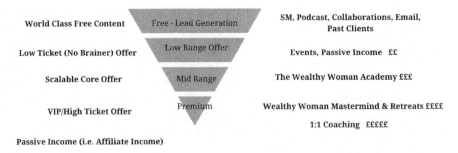

World Class Free Content	Free - Lead Generation	SM, Podcast, Collaborations, Email, Past Clients
Low Ticket (No Brainer) Offer	Low Range Offer	Events, Passive Income ££
Scalable Core Offer	Mid Range	The Wealthy Woman Academy £££
VIP/High Ticket Offer	Premium	Wealthy Woman Mastermind & Retreats ££££
		1:1 Coaching £££££

Passive Income (i.e. Affiliate Income)

The level of results, energy needed to execute and proximity needs to also reflect this model

All of these offers can be supported by a team or tech to enable you to stay in your zone of genius & do what you do best

LEVEL 1 – WORLD CLASS, FREE CONTENT

If you want to attract world class, Unicorn clients, who will throw their credit cards at you, you need to create world-class free content to demonstrate what a badass you are first. Put out rubbish, half-arsed 'filler' content, that doesn't activate your audience, showcase what a leader you are, give value, or position you as the perfect solution to their problem, and you will attract needy clients, that need their objections 'handling' in response.

I don't know about you, but the thought of convincing people to let me help them, or needing to manipulate them into a purchase does not feel good to me. I once had a coach that used such dated sales strategies, that she advised me to encourage my clients to apply for credit cards and insist on non-refundable deposit payments to be taken on all my sales calls.

Talk about a scarcity mindset. She obviously felt that without pressure and manipulation, she wasn't good enough to be invested in. When the fear creeps in, take a moment to ask yourself, 'what am I making this situation mean about me as a person right now?'.

I would prefer my clients to work with me when they are excited to do so, rather than scared or under pressure. The energetic exchange, and the results that will be created are truly on a different level.

Repeat after me, THERE ARE ALWAYS MORE CLIENTS!

Creating content that plays to your natural strengths is a must, to make it fun and aligned. As mentioned, I'm a high vibe chatty Cathy, so a podcast, filled with collaborations (that play to my super connector superpower) and entertaining video content is a no-brainer.

Make sure that whatever you are putting out, is your truth and not what you feel you should say. It's ok to repel some of your audience, only 10% are ever going to buy from your anyway. Better to make sure that those 10% are YOUR people, who love the unapologetic, hot-mess, high-integrity, big hearted version of you, then a carefully curated social media persona, that leaves you out of alignment whenever you jump on a call.

LEVEL 2 – LOW TICKET, NO BRAINER OFFERS ££

These are the offers that act as a 'gateway drug' to your bigger offers. Perhaps they are the first part of a much bigger puzzle, so once completed, the next logical step is to ascend to your higher ticket offer, once they have some quick results under their belt.

These offers are great, as they typically don't require much faith or trust, to invest in, and the risk is perceived to be particularly low. These offers can be easily pulled together by repurposing content that you have already created. They can also be set up to host passively, with a funnel to support a nurture sequence of emails that can then encourage your clients to upsell into your higher ticket offers.

Mini-courses, workbooks, E-books, audio bundles can be great low-ticket offers. I have a Dream Life Workbook that I created as a tool for my clients, that I put onto Amazon, for a truly passive income and it still generates monthly sales for me, two years after I created it. Finding smart ways to receive an income, without having an energy exchange needed is the key to scaling your business in the most sustainable way.

LEVEL 3 – SCALABLE SIGNATURE OFFER £££

You need to have a scalable offer, that allows you to serve multiple clients at one time. This could be a group program, academy, membership, mastermind, large-scale events, or self-study program with an added community element.

This becomes the main offer that you promote, and where all your energy goes into selling. Clients that you attract can either be upsold into your High-Ticket offer, if they want closer proximity or a VIP experience, or down sold into your lower ticket offers, if they are not yet ready to invest.

This is how you truly start to experience the time freedom available to you as a business owner. This model works well, if what you are selling is good, and you maintain boundaries by not overdelivering outside of the container. Even if it's tempting to, it completely negates the purpose of the offer. If you can grow your scalable offer, you will have more time to create better content, master your sales process and step into your CEO self. My offer is my Wealthy Woman Academy. Because I have this main point of focus, this has become my spiritual home and the place I pour all of my money evolution goodness into.

The world wins when you think bigger and allow yourself to serve at a higher level.

For me, with your scalable offer, you should also increase the duration of this offer to 6 to 12 months to:

A – Increase flexibility for your clients, by being able to offer monthly instalment payment plans, to make this offer as accessible as possible

B – Increase stability in your business, by adding monthly reoccurring revenue from your payment plans

C – Increase the level of transformation or experience for your client, by keeping them inside your world, and community, for longer.

Winner, winner, winner.

Often when I see women in a hustle state in their business, it's because they are not creating containers that last long enough. This is usually because they are trying to keep their costs 'accessible' to the clients that they believe cannot afford them. They undervalue their client's ability to be resourceful and find a way to make things happen when they want a desired outcome. This puts them under pressure to deliver results quickly, means they are always left trying to find the 'next client' and can usually only scratch the surface of what magic they can create with their clients, if only they had more time to do so.

It also creates unrealistic expectations of their clients, from the get-go, when they are sold the dream of quick results. I have found, it's better to speak to the value of long-term mentorship, gradual growth, and sustainable success, than promise quick wins and fast cash. That form of 'bro' marketing only attracts the wrong kind of clients, for whom, free will never be free enough.

LEVEL 4 – PREMIUM OFFER ££££/£

In any offer suite, you need to allow the people who can pay more, to pay more, and receive a better service or experience in exchange. This doesn't mean that you shortchange your other clients, but that you have something reserved that feels aspirational and more bespoke than your other offers.

As a coach or service provider, it could be an exclusive mastermind or 1:1 offer that gives your clients closer proximity access to you, and or your team. If you have a product-based business, this could be your core offer or product but with bells on. Even Amazon gives customers the option of next day delivery if they want to pay more for it. Those that don't will wait, it's their choice. Don't feel bad about charging more for your highest proximity offers, you have your scalable offer for those that are not ready to invest at that level. My premium offers are my Wealthy Woman Mastermind and my Wealthy Woman Retreat, which are both luxurious, intimate and incredibly fun to deliver. The focus is moved away from the HOW questions that relate to money and business, and focussed more on the EMBODIMENT of feminine leadership. These tables and rooms are where the conversations are focussed on changing industries, creating bigger impacts, expanding missions, collaborations, building wealth and contributing to societal causes at a higher level. You can find details on my website about when the doors open next, for both.

Often, I see women selling their holy grail, most precious resource-based offers (their own personal time and energy) as if it were some bargain basement offer, when the reality is the reverse. Not everyone should have access to your ability to hand hold them through a process or a journey and that's ok.

I have found that creating this stackable offer suite, where each offer feels like an upgrade on the last, has helped my heart-centred clients reconcile their prices. They no longer feel cheeky or audacious, by charging high ticket for their 1:1 offers, because they know they have other places to send prospective clients if they are unable to invest at that level. This means they can hold their boundaries around their offers, have more conviction in selling each offer, always ensure any client leaves with a solution that matches their needs and budget, and make sure that they never leave money on the table again. It also increases their lifetime value of their clients, as they continue to stay in your world and graduate through your offers. I have clients that have been with me for over 5 years, which literally makes my heart happy, that as I grow, they grow with me.

LEVEL 5 – PASSIVE & AFFILIATE INCOME

Whatever business model you have, some elements of your sales and delivery needs to be somewhat passive or you will struggle to make the bigger impact that you crave.

Low ticket offers, attached to funnels, are a great way of doing that. Affiliate income is another great income too. Affiliate income is where you become an affiliate for someone else's business and receive a commission for any referrals or recommendations that you facilitate. This can be as easy or hard as you want it to be.

If you use software and love it, become an affiliate of that business. I receive thousands a month in affiliate income, and most companies will offer an incentive for referrals. I am a Kajabi expert, and love to use it with my clients, when setting up their businesses. If they then choose to invest, it's only right that I receive a small payment for that referral.

This is because, if someone has personally recommended a person or a thing to someone else, they are far more likely to invest in that thing too. This makes it an easier and probably more aligned sale for the business, who is likely to commit long term to their offer. Win win all round. It's nice to be nice, but it's also nice to be paid!

As mentioned, I have referred six figures of business to other Women in Business, in the last 12 months alone – Have I received referrals from those women in return – NOPE! Did I make sure that I received an affiliate commission for most of those referrals? Hell Yes!

It's an energy exchange, and I deserve to be compensated for it. Anything that comes up for you, that tells you it's bad or wrong to want that exchange, is a limiting money belief, and an invitation to explore further with your journal.

Having a stackable offer suite is the best way to ensure:

- Every prospective client has a solution for their problem, at whatever price-point and proximity feels aligned to them.

- You can scale your business and remain in your CEO role, working ON your business, rather than continually IN your business, exchanging your time for money.

- You keep clients in your world for longer, giving them a clear pathway mapped out, and next level of offer that they can either ascend to or descend to, if they no longer need the close proximity. It's not about how many clients you have, but what you are doing with them, that matters.

- You never leave money on the table again or miss an opportunity to fuel your business with sales, as you have a clear line of sight of which offer to sell to the right client at the right point in their journey.

- You build your monthly reoccurring revenue in your business, rather than focussing on high-cash sales months. MRR is the real flex in business, as is knowing that you have your bills covered till the following year, regardless of whether life throws you a curveball, you get sick, or want to take some time off.

There has been a huge focus on the £10k month, as the holy grail for business owners. Do you need £10k months, to have a damn successful business, and fulfilling life or is this an arbitrary measure of success that one person created, and is now accepted as a win?

For me the real flex is consistent, sustainable, stackable revenue that grows month on month. No one ever got to £100k months by starting from zero every month on the first. They used they're already existing MRR to leverage, and stack on top of, from a place of desire rather than need. This allows them to regulate their nervous system, make better decisions and take bolder action, knowing that their basic needs are met.

4 – A Commitment to Getting Visible AF

I love me some Grant Cardone and when he said '*If they don't know you, they can't flow you*' it firstly made me chuckle, but it gave me a lightbulb moment too. Grant Cardone is a property tycoon and business mentor, that encourages aggressive promotion and omnipresence, to making as much money as possible for your business.

Not everyone is trying to create a 7-figure empire, but there are great reasons as to why that goal should be a thing. As mentioned in the first few chapters, the world needs YOU to be wealthy, so that you can make it a better place. Wealthy does not mean hustling month to month, trying to find the next client or pay your bills. Wealthy means thriving in all areas of life, so that you can be abundant and in overflow, and help others around you. There is no point you essentially having the most incredible offer on the planet and keeping it yourself for fear of being judged or seen as too salesy.

I get it, being 'seen' can be scary. Facing judgment can be scary, and it goes against all our natural instincts to 'fit in', be a good girl, and be accepted by those around us. But someone out there, in this moment is in pain, because they don't know that you exist or that you can help them. This perspective has gotten me out of my own way, many times over the years when I fell down a rabbit hole of self-doubt and perfectionism. 'It's not about me, it's about HER', was a mantra that went round and round in my head, whenever I needed a moment to get out of my own way.

It's about the woman who is struggling to make the income she deserves, because she doesn't know how, and is about to quit and return to corporate.
It's about the woman who is letting fear, failure and self-doubt consume her, and keep her from her greatness.

It's about the woman who is hustling, trying to be a good person, doing all the things, burning herself out, and exhausted.

It's about the woman who is accepting shizzle from others, allowing people to push her round, and overstep their boundaries, because she doesn't feel empowered to say no.

It's about the woman who has an ache in her heart, at the mission and vision she has for her business but has no idea where to start.

We are the generation that will change the game for our daughters, and the generations to come.

We get to set the new normal, change the views of society and redefine what success looks like, on our own damn terms. But only when we get out of our own way, and commit to getting visible AF, regardless of the judgement that may come our way. This is why I create communities around each of my offers, because being a trailblazer can be hard, and lonely, and being amongst a tribe of women who get it, is priceless.

Increasing Your Pathways to be Paid

I couldn't finish this book, without sharing one more strategy that will support you in getting the most financial bang for your buck, if you have a service-based business. I didn't want to include it in the previous chapter, as it can get confusing when you have too many options available to you, to fully monetise your business. A confused mind always stays stuck, so only read on if you consider yourself more of an advanced business owner, who is ready to stack the cash and has assets to repurpose.

One of the reasons that I am known as The Queen of Leverage is because I have mastered the art of monetisation and fully optimising any business to its fullest. Even when I was younger, I was always that friend who knew the credit cards with the best interest rates, the sites that give you the most cashback, the retailers that give you the best loyalty points and the best off-set mortgages to invest in.

Money has always fascinated me, in a playful way, and I have always been curious as to how you can make it go further. I want to share with you how I have monetised my signature wealth activation program, The Millionaire Mindset Bootcamp, 13 different ways, since I originally created it 3 years ago.

My hope is that this will inspire you, to fill any gaps in your customer journey, and see your business assets as 'assets' that can be the gift that keeps on giving. I don't want to overwhelm you, or overcomplicate your business, but instead create a commercial awareness around the magic that you have already within your business.

I also want to say, that I haven't monetised my program creatively, because I am solely focussed on creating a shed ton of money. I am a Manifesting Generator and we need to be able to move quickly in business. If I continued to deliver the same content contained within this program, live, the energy would dissipate, and it wouldn't be as fun to deliver.

The do however continually add to the program by creating new modules, but the basic principles remain the same. I am not a rinse and repeat kinda girl, so this is me staying in my zone of genius. The upside for anyone who invests in this incredible program, is that it is the gift that keeps on giving, as once you invest once, you have lifetime access to all the additions and upgrades. To find out more details visit my website – www.thefemalepreneurcoach.co.uk/millionaire-mindset-bootcamp.

There are the ways in which I have continued to monetise this program, and expand my pathways to be paid:

1 – I ran the original program live which gave me my first stream of income from the program. I would always advise this, so that you can make tweaks and improvements along the way. I am a big fan of creating in collaboration with my community, so that I can ensure I am delivering on what they need.

2 – I also gave people the option to increase their purchase price with a VIP Upsell. This included an additional bonus 1:1 session with me to dive deeper into their own personal money blocks. Whether you are creating a low-ticket offer, or even free, ALWAYS GIVE A VIP UPSELL option, and allow those who want to pay more, for an enhanced experience, to pay more.

3 – I repackaged the program as a self-study, which still creates a monthly income Today. I also added monthly instalment options, to honour the value of the original program, while making it as accessible as possible, to anyone who wanted to really *do the work* and transform their relationship with money. You could even add an upsell to your own program and allow people to add on a 1:1 strategy session with you, like I did in the original live program.

4 - I took individual modules and sold them as low-ticket paid masterclasses, which then acted as a lead magnet for the main program, as most people upsold into the full bootcamp afterwards.

5 – I took individual modules and presented those as paid guest expert sessions in other people's groups and masterminds. You could also do paid speaker stage work, based on your program's key concepts, and learning points.

6 – I created a mini-version of the program, recorded as an audio-series called Millionaire Mindset Mumma and sold that as a lower ticket offer, in audible form only. I could have literally just retracted the audio files from the original program, as I filmed it in zoom, but I wanted to tailor the content towards Mums, as opposed to WIB. You can purchase it here if you are interested – www.thefemalepreneurcoach.co.uk/millionaire-mindset-mumma

7 – I bundled the program with my signature business building academy, The Aligned, Empowered & Abundant Academy, as a tripwire upsell offer when people purchased the program, to increase conversions

8 – I added it as a down-sell to other programs if people were not ready to invest at the higher level.

9 – I extracted the resources used throughout the program and bundled as a hypnosis audio series. My clients have also done this, as a way of allowing people to 'try before they buy'.

10 – I used it as a bonus to increase conversions on my other, higher ticket offers. This is a great strategy when launching new programs.

11 – I used the framework of the bootcamp, to write this book, which will hopefully be a future best-seller. If you are holding this book right now, please take this as your friendly nudge from me and The Universe, to write your glowing Amazon review, so that I can reach more incredible women like you! You could also distil your program contents in a book or e-book and pop onto Amazon too, as a low-ticket lead magnet into your higher ticket offers.

12 – I added an affiliate commission, to allow others to sell my program on my behalf and receive an affiliate commission in return. This works well for clients, who have their own clients with issues around their money mindset. They appear to be super helpful, and can help their clients on multiple levels, by selling them my course, and in exchange their client receives an incredible experience, and uplevel in their money, and they receive a commission as a thank you. Win, win all round!

13 – I offer VIP Intensive sessions, for clients that want to dive deeper than ever into their relationship with money and create a personalised monetisation blueprint for their business. This is sold at a premium price, because it is an intimate experience, that literally transforms lives, and creates massive uplevels in success.

Journal Prompt:

What assets or content, can you repurpose to fully optimise your income and increase your pathways to be paid?

Pricing 101

One of the biggest struggles I see with new clients, is how to price their services. As mentioned, before there seems to be three approaches to pricing that are most common amongst women:

1 – The low-ball approach. Thinking that cheap means easy to sell, women low-ball their prices to a point of unsustainability, and keeps them firmly placed in the hustle, flying by the seat of your pants mode, which is not fun at all.

2 – Crowd-sourcing your prices. Either asking everyone around you, your audience, your friends, dog, and neighbours what they think it is worth, or googling the average prices of your competitors (who are probably dealing with their own money shizzle) and sticking with what seems reasonable.

3 – The Audacious AF approaches. Demanding high-ticket prices because someone told you, you could, regardless of your experience, commitment to mastery or the results that you have created for your clients. I once had a coach who told me I could easily triple my prices, when I asked why, he replied 'because you can'. I appreciated the gaslighting but couldn't shake the feeling that I would become part of the problem, if I increased my prices not based on my performance, but because some sucker would inevitably pay it.

Here is my no B.S. approach to pricing your services, with integrity, so that you feel good doing it, and don't have to compromise any part of your soul in the process:

Do:

- Focus on what the outcome/result/experience is worth to your ideal client. What would they give, to be where you are right now? If your skills have the potential to make your clients £50k, why are you charging a tenner for it?

- Recognise that money is a fuel that is needed to grow your business, and that everyone wins when your prices are sustainable.

- Consider your own investments, time and energy, that you have put into mastering your craft. I often see incredibly heart-led healers, who have spent years refining their gifts, to then sell them at a pittance, which keeps them in a toxic hustle cycle.

- Consider the tangible and intangible costs of executing on your offers. Yes, it might just be your personal time and energy, but that has a cost, and you deserve to be compensated.

- Ensure there is a balance of expectations. You cannot charge high-ticket prices for a subpar offer. One of my biggest frustrations is when I see people market their offers as Masterminds, because they believe that they can charge high-ticket for it, when they are delivering nothing more than a high-ticket group coaching program. I believe it's better to exceed expectations, and over deliver, so you can increase your lifetime value (LTV) of your clients and chance of referrals.

- Make sure that all your prices make sense, when put together. I once had a client who had unwittingly charged the same price for 1:1 service, as they had to the VIP Members of their Mastermind. Not all money is equal however, the cost of a 1:1 client is a lot higher energetically, as you must energetically hold space for that person. For a small reduction income, but no extra work at all, it makes sense to funnel clients into your scalable offer or make your 1:1 service A LOT higher, so the exchange makes sense.

Don't:

- Negate your previous experience, or transferrable skills that you bring to the table, even if you are new to an industry. You don't have to 'earn your stripes' before you can earn a good living, yes even if it doesn't feel like work at all.

- Allow industry averages to guide you. Everyone has their own money shizzle they are dealing with, and there is a client for every price-point. Gucci doesn't look at Primark to compare prices, Gucci owns the fact that it's Gucci, and not everyone will be able to afford them, and they keep it moving.

- Create a business model that relies on a high volume of sales, unless you have a budget for ad spend.

- Take rejection personally or make it about you. It's ok to not be accessible to everyone, that's where the smart offer suite comes into play. I have had lots of potential clients tell me that working with me 1:1 is on their vision board and that literally makes my heart happy, because when they get there, the satisfaction and feeling of accomplishment is going to be incredible!

- Feel the need to add lots of bonuses to your offers, to reinforce the value that you are charging. It's either worth it, or it isn't, and no number of distracting bonuses will compensate for that. 'The program was massively overpriced, but at least I got some great Canva templates' said no-one.

Journal Prompt:

Considering the dos and don'ts above, how do your current prices stack up?

Where do you need to increase your prices, or reduce your proximity and bonuses?

Where do you need to reconcile your pricing, so no one offer negates from another?

STRATEGY
- MONEY MANAGEMENT

Moving From Vision - What Does Your Dream Life Cost?

When it comes to money, it's not always how much money you receive, but the intentionality you have around what you are doing with it, that counts.

And yet, a report released by the Fawcett Society, reveals that only 40% of women are likely to have a good level of financial education, as opposed to 67% of men. We already know from our earlier chapters, as to the reasoning as to why this might be. The sad truth is, it's more important than ever for women to feel confident in their finances and be able to advocate for themselves and their needs.

This is due to so many economic and social reasons such as increasing pressure to contribute to household bills, and the fact that women live longer than men, but are far less likely to have any sort of retirement fund to support them in their senior years.

First, I must set a disclaimer – I am not a financial planner or advisor, and I cannot give you specific advice on where to put your money, to get the highest returns on your investments. I can however share with you my common sense, basic B approach to money management, that has supported myself and my clients in maximising our financial power.

So.. In the words of the Spice Girls – *Tell me what you want, what you really, really want?*

When you think of your dream life, the most boujee (or not), abundant life, where you live entirely on your own terms, and get to explore every passion and interest, how much do you believe that it will cost?

Chances are, it's not as much as you think!

When I first did this exercise, I was shocked at how possible my dream life was. I had assumed I would need millions, when in fact I needed far less.

If I had a pound for every client that comes to me, to support them in their search of the holy grail of online service providers – the £10k month, I would have £10k months in reoccurring revenue just from those clients alone! Women are tying themselves up in knots, trying to hit arbitrary income goals, to buy things they don't really want, but believe will validate them, so they can live a life they don't want.

Often when I start working with clients, they are still very much moving and making decisions, based on their current circumstances, even though it isn't where they want to be. It reminds me of that age-old saying 'if you always do, what you always did, you will always get, what you always got'. I encourage myself clients instead, to move from vision. If you have a big picture goal, rather than delaying that goal and make it become the never-ending goalpost, why you start to act, think, and move from that place now.

My first invitation to you is to take a moment to sit with your hand on your heart, quieten your mind and consider what your dream life looks like.

Who is with you?

Where do you live?

How do you spend your days?

What is your level of self-care like?

What does your week look like?

Where do you go on holiday, and how frequently?

What are your hobbies?

How much do you have in your bank accounts, savings accounts, investments?

What do you invest in?

What support do you have at home and in your business?

If you struggle to visualise your dream life, there is a powerful 'Stepping Into Your Future Self' Meditation that will help, in the book resources section of my website – www.thefemalepreneurcoach.co.uk/bookresources.

The intention of this exercise is to create a vision so compelling and magnetic, that it literally pulls you forward, and into inspired action mode, so that you can manifest it quicker. When we have big, audacious goals, we can easily get overwhelmed with the enormity of the task and end up frozen in place.

We end up taking no action at all, or take some action at first, which gradually dissipates as we realise, we still have such a long way to go. We can also, fall guilty of taking token action steps because that future feels so far away in the distance. We give ourselves an 'out', believing that one day in 5 years' time we are going to wake up and be living the life of our dreams.

The reality is, it's the small, incremental, daily action steps that you take, that will either move you closer to your dream life or take you further away. Remember, if nothing changes, NOTHING CHANGES.

The clearer you can get on what your dream life looks and feels like, the easier it will be to notice the gaps in how you are showing up and behaving in your current life now. It also helps you to lessen the resistance your unconscious mind will have towards that goal, as we already know it has an inherent fear of the unknown. The more you can get familiar, and into the detail of what that future life looks like, the more things will seemingly fall into place, with ease, to create it.

There are a few approaches you can take to get really clear on the details of your dream life:

- Brainstorm your bucket list for the next 2/5/10 years and timeline all the things you would like to achieve or create within those milestones.

- Listen to the 'Future Self' meditation and then journal on the gaps between where you currently are in life, and where you want to be. If you're Future Self goes to Yoga once a week, take a symbolic step forward, and book yourself a yoga lesson Today. If you can't afford yoga lessons yet, take the next best step and commit to regular at home sessions with free resources from You Tube.

- List out of your Future Self expenses, and put them onto a spreadsheet, so you can get a realistic picture of what your monthly costs will be, it might surprise you and be more accessible than you think. Usually, we talk ourselves out of dreaming too big, as we assume everything is way out of our league.

  The reality is rich people are not walking into an expensive car dealership and paying in cash $250,000 for a Lamborghini in full. It would be a waste of their capital, as it would depreciate as soon as they drove it away from the dealership. Chances are, like us, they would lease the car and pay in monthly instalments – how much would those be? Create a monthly budget for all the things that you truly desire, such as holidays, gifts, special occasions, self-development, team costs etc.

  Have fun, getting into the detail, and remember this is your most abundant life. This is about feeling abundant in all areas of your life, and not just about how many handbags you want to budget for on your shopping trips.

- Think about how you want to spend a typical day in your new abundant life, and write a letter to your Future Self, dated at a significant point in the future, when you have already accomplished everything that you wanted. Really drop down into your body and connect all your senses to this vision of your perfect day in the future. Again, it may surprise you. I did this exercise, expecting to see myself at a luxury New York apartment, and I was at the beach, watching my kids play. It made me realise that my ambition was no longer the main driving force for my business, as I had nothing left to prove to anyone else, but the quality of life and time I wanted to spend with my kids.

  This awareness has shaped every business decision since that moment. Family is one of my core values, and rather than being an afterthought, it's one of my main driving values to everything that I do.

Now that you have a clear picture of the kind of life you would like to create, it's time to start moving from that vision,

Practically

Psychologically

Financially

Strategically

Energetically

I'm going to dive a little deeper into each concept.

Practically

Bad news - the only thing that stands in the way of your dream life, is You.

Good news – the only thing that stands in the way of your dream life is You! The relationship that you have with money is symbolic of what you feel worthy and safe of receiving. This relationship will also be showing up in other areas of your life. If you feel that your money is chaotic and unreliable, chances are there are other areas of your life that also feel chaotic (kitchen drawers, handbags, time management etc.) and unreliable too. It's time to get intentional with all areas of your life, friendship groups, boundaries, how you are spending your time, what you are saying yes to, basically all the things.

Firstly, how are you spending your time right now? Are you running around, prioritising everyone else's needs but your own, trapped in a mindset that you NEED to do these things? Are you spending time with people that you no longer feel aligned to, but feel like you can't say no? Are you telling yourself that to be a good Mum, that you can only work on your business, when the kids are not around, or need to restrict the number of hours that you work?

Are you wasting time and energy that you could be working on your business, and earning an income, on low value tasks like doing food shops (that could easily be switched to online delivery), cleaning your bathroom (that could be outsourced to a cleaner, when you consider your potential hourly income rate vs a professional cleaner) or offering too many free coffee chats, to potential clients?

Worn Out Woman Boundaries	Wealthy Woman Boundaries
I don't want to go to coffee with Susan, she always moans, and I end up feeling really drained. I end up giving her a free therapy session and she never pays for coffee.	I only surround myself with people that light me up and fuel my passion, not energy vampires that drain me.
I have a load of commitments in my diary, that I really don't want to do, but must. Even though they eat into the time I could be working on my business, increasing my self-development, or researching ways to invest my money.	I choose to say No to the things that don't light me up or add value to my life. It's ok to not be seen as a good person for honouring my own boundaries, as now I can do something that I want to do instead.
I know they can't afford my services, but I'll hop on a free call anyway, as I want to be a good person and help everyone.	My free content is so valuable that I am going to direct them to my resources instead. When they have some quick wins under their belt, and can afford to invest in my programs, I will jump onto connection calls if needed. It's ok to not be accessible 24/7 to everyone who wants to speak to me or pick my brains.
I don't know what I'm doing or where I'm going wrong so I'll sign up for every free challenge and lead-magnet, which will leave me more confused than ever (If I actually show up and use them), and stuck from taking action	I will be resourceful at ensuring the mentorship or training that I need to create my next level of success. Even if I need to wait, or put intentional savings plans in place, I can make things happen when I know it's what I want.

Everyone is saying that there is a cost-of-living crisis, and no one is buying right now, so I'll lower my income expectations, or my prices and lean out from my business.	I create my own economy and know that there are billions of people in the world, and I only need a small fraction to buy from me to have a great business. I only surround myself with people that speak positively about money and remind me what is possible for me too.
I am scared to invest money into my business, what if I don't make it back?	I trust myself to make smart financial decisions, even if things I have invested into before didn't work out. I know there is always more abundance and more clients available to me at any time.
I'm focussed on growing my business.	I'm focussed on scaling my business, and ensuring it can run without me.
I need to add everything and the kitchen sink to my offers to convince people to buy, in-case I can't find any other clients.	I know the value I bring to the table for my clients, and there are always more clients, and there are always easier ways to make money.
Even though I don't enjoy doing certain tasks in my business, and I am not an expert of the best person to be doing it, I will give it a go as it saves me money from paying an expert to do it instead.	I understand where my value is in my business, and that wasting my time doing things I have no business doing, is limiting my growth and potential income. I am happy to invest in people who can do it better, quicker, and more professionally.

Psychologically

We have already discovered how your beliefs about money are impacting your mindset today and affecting your actions and your income. Seeing first hand, how the different sides of my family spoke and acted around money, really cemented for me the logic as to why some of them were abundant than others.

I have captured the differences between the poor and the rich money mindsets below, take stock of how many you relate to on each side of the table:

Worn Out Woman Mindset	Wealthy Woman Mindset
I need to focus on cutting my expenses, and to save money	I can only get my expenses down to zero, but my earning potential is unlimited, I focus more on bringing more money in

Making money is hard, and needs lots of complicated elements to my business, or a huge team to support me	Making money is easy, the simpler my business model, the more I can make.
No-one is buying right now, better try and cut back, while there is a cost-of-living crisis	There are billions of people in the world and millions who can benefit from my services
I feel personally let down or attacked by money	I feel neutral about money and know it's just an exchange of energy
I can't collaborate with other women; they might try and steal my clients	There are more than enough clients for everyone.
I wait for a crisis to happen before getting resourceful to pay my bills	I proactively use this resourceful energy to create an overflow of money, and savings that can support me if I need it
Focussed on paying next month's bills	Focussing on 5-year goals and plans
Focussed on making money	Focussed on building long-term, generational wealth
Trades their time for money – I work for money	Leverages their money to create wealth – money works for me
Believes life is happening to them, and feel powerless to change their financial situation	Knows life is happening from them, and that they have the power to change their situation at any time
Focusses on what will logically make them money	Focusses on what they love, and knows they will find a way to monetise it
The more success you have, the more problems you have	The more success you have, the more can you be supported
Focusses on saving	Focusses on investing
Buys designer bags to validate their self-worth and status to other people	Invests in their personal development and radiates badass confidence
Wanting more than you need is greedy and ungrateful	Everyone wins when I win

One of my favourite quotes about the wealthy woman mindset, came from a lady that I met in LA at a luxury retreat with 6.7 and 8 figure business owners. When I asked her, 'what do you think the difference is between the poor and the rich, she said '*The poor stay poor by acting rich, and the rich stay rich by acting poor*'.

It blew my mind because I was that person for a moment. When I first started making real money in my business, I spent it like I stole it. I was trying to position myself as a badass CEO, who brunches at boujee places and wears designer shoes, to validate my decision to back myself.

99

I had had friends who thought I was crazy, ex-colleagues who had laughed at me behind my back, and I felt like I had the world and its wife just waiting for me to fail. Rather than building my own self-confidence trust and resilience, I tried to silence them with designer purchases that I wore as armour, to protect myself from their judgement.

It wasn't until I recognised these toxic relationships that I had surrounded myself with, because I wanted them to love me, and focussed on building up my own self-love, did I start to create changes. It was like I was looking for approval from the mean girls at school, who really didn't want to see me win, and it was a never-ending cycle of shame.

I have recorded a podcast episode on this very topic, if you want to dive in deeper, called 'What to do when other people aren't supporting your success'. You can find it, wherever you listen to your podcasts, such as Apple and Spotify. I also have another podcast episode on how to deal with other's people shizzle around money, when you are trying to uplevel your own. A lot of the time I work with clients, who are ready to do the work, and uplevel their lives, but have partners, friends and relatives who aren't in the same place, and it affects them energetically.

Financially

As a business owner, an absolute must read, when it comes to managing your cash flow, within your business is Mike Michalowicz's book, Profit First. It was a complete eye-opener for me.

Up until this point, I was happy to take pennies from my business, while it grew. As my staff went on expensive holidays, I stayed at home with my kids. My understanding of profit was that you had your income, minus expenses, and that equalled the profit that was available to you. Mike's book flips the script on that theory and supports you to manage your cash flow proactively, by deciding how much profit you want to create FIRST. You would then take your income, minus the profit that you want, and this leaves the amount of money that is available for your operating expenses.

Often, we can end up over-investing, under-investing or being wildly unrealistic with how much money we need to make. This approach helps you to get a sensible approach to income expectations, and assures that you get paid first, not last, regardless of your sales that month.

Taking this one step further, I always encourage my clients to intentionally plan that their income is allocated in the following ratios:

50% for their personal expenses and taxes

20% Investments (unless you have high interest debts, in which case prioritise getting those paid off should be a priority, consider them a leaky bucket otherwise)

10% Savings and low interest debts (always pay over your minimum repayments, to save paying more in the long run than you need to)

10% Fun and guilt-free purchases

10% Retirement and legacy

If their current income doesn't support these ratios, then they need to either reconsider their expenses or earn more money!

When it comes to your expenses, I have the philosophy that you should spend big on the things you love, without guilt or shame, and mercilessly cut out or reduce the things that you really aren't that bothered about.

Equally there will be expenses that cannot go, in which case you need to find a way to feel good about them, so that you don't allow underlying resentment towards them, lower your vibration.

Examples below:

Keep	Cut	Reframe
Netflix subscription that you love and use every day.	Gym membership that you have no intention of utilising but feel bad about cancelling.	Rent payment that is annoyingly high – Reframe: I am so grateful to have a beautiful home that is mine, and a safe space to lay my head every night. I am grateful to live in a nice neighbourhood that commands high rents.
Your morning coffee that lights you up and feels like Christmas.	The supermarket sandwich at lunchtime that is convenient but tastes like cardboard.	Extortionate petrol prices – I am so grateful to have my own car that can take me wherever I want to go, in the most efficient way.

The beautiful outfit you purchased for a night out, that you cannot wait to wear.	The impulse tatt from Poundland that you really don't need or care about.	High VAT or Tax bills – Evey penny earned in my business represents someone's life that I have made better in some way. High taxes remind me of the bigger impact that I am having in the world.

Inside my Wealthy Woman Academy, I have countless resources, that will support you in setting up good money management systems inside and outside of your business. The key is to spend intentionally, ensuring that you are spending every penny consciously, and with joy.

Wealth Creation

I always encourage my clients to be thinking long term when it comes to their business finances. This means prioritising building Monthly Reoccurring Revenue (MRR), through extended payment plans, longer term offers and the ability to pay in instalments.

For me right now, I know that my bills are paid until next August, whether I sell another offer or do another thing. As a Mum with 5 kids, who is prone to a few life curveballs, this gives me the confidence I need to A – sleep at night, B – make bolder decisions and take bigger action, knowing my basic needs are met, and C – move from vision rather than short term needs. Trust me, your whole vibe is different, you make very different decisions and protect your boundaries like a Mumma bear, when you know your basic needs are met.

When other business coaches are glamourising high cash months and £100k launches, I encourage my clients to focus on building their MRR through scalable offers, so they can run their life and businesses on their owns, from a place of safety. That is the real flex for me.

Once you have an overflow of income, I strongly encourage you to look at smart ways to invest that money into wealth building strategies that will give you a return on your investment. Identifying the most aligned strategies is one of the things that I support my clients with inside my high-level mastermind – The Wealthy Woman Mastermind. I have brought in guest experts in Stocks and Shares portfolios, Property Experts, Tax Efficiency Accountants and more, to support the women to leverage their business profits.

This enables them to focus on creating true legacy, rich-lady wealth, that will support themselves and their families for years to come. It is now easier than ever to start a small investment portfolio for yourself, thanks to online apps and resources. You no longer need to feel intimidated or overwhelmed or have buy-in figures to act as a barrier to getting started.

My client started their own Stocks and Shares portfolio using an app, with just £5 a week and already sees a consistent 8% return on her investments, which are compounding by the day. As I mentioned before, it is the small, incremental, consistent actions steps that you take each day, that are ultimately going to get you to your dream life. I believe in quantum leaps too, but if every day you are intentionally taking steps to move you closer to your dream life, rather than away from it, those are positive inspired action steps too. We never want to be stuck in 'waiting energy', i.e., waiting for a high-cash month to put something aside for savings, do it now, even if it's only £5 – it's symbolic and is still moving you closer to your dream life.

Strategically

This is creating a business model and offer suite that allows you to stack cash, and increase your revenue streams and client Lifetime Value (LTV), whilst also being proactive in building your investments and savings.

It means setting yourself up for the most likely outcome of success. I like to call this creating environment for success. I love the quote *'If a Rose fails to bloom, you don't change the rose, you change the environment'*, and the same is true for you.

Are you being honest with how much time you need to work on your business, or are you trying to hustle with your laptop balancing on your knee, while trying to answer calls and do a million other things at once?

Are you surrounding yourself with the right people, who can support you with your growth? Are you in the right rooms, and at the right tables? Your net-worth is in your network after all, and you are the sum of the 5 people you spend the most amount of time with.

Are you investing in your own self-development and being supported by mentors who can short-cut your success?

Are you boot-strapping your business and trying to save pennies, which is causing you to leave significant money-making opportunities on the table?

Are you spending every day starting from scratch, with no plan to follow, so you are left throwing spaghetti at the wall, when it comes to growing your business?

Energetically

Money loves a purpose, and to feel desired. Connect with your dream life vision and get clear on the numbers and what you need to make it a reality.

Make space for new abundance. If you want more clients, do you have capacity to serve more clients?

Do you need to build a more scalable offer, get help at home, or increase your prices so you can serve more clients at a better price-point? Equally, if you are trying to manifest money for a shopping spree, do you have space in your wardrobe for more clothes, or is already stuffed full of low-cost outfits that don't fit well, or make you feel excited? Are you accepting metaphorical scraps, because they are better than nothing, and you are worried about being to afford to replace them?

One thing I love to do inside my programs is a weekly or monthly Money Date. This is where you:

A - Intentionally go through all your finances and ensure everything that is being spent, is done with intention, purpose and love.

B - You identify opportunities to make more money, by leveraging your assets and converting them into passive income streams or taking overflow and funnelling it into investment opportunities.

C – You forgive anything that has come up around money that week, that makes you feel negatively about it. You then let go of the negative hold it has over you and creates energetic space to make more money.

Conclusion

I am writing this conclusion sat next to a stunning roof-top pool, inside a fabulous hotel in Beverly Hills, LA, at which I am currently staying. The sun is shining, I have a cocktail by my side, and I couldn't feel more abundant right now.

Not only because the hotel is located just off Rodeo drive, known for its designer stores and wealth, but because the views of the Hollywood hills are an expansive and breathtaking reminder of just how abundant the Universe is. Everything in LA just radiates 'possibility'. The person you are standing next to in line at the coffee shop is just as likely to be a celebrity or a tech millionaire than a regular person, with a 9-5 job.

I booked this trip intentionally, as a symbolic gesture, when I wanted to finish writing this book. There is no better way, to get into, and embody the feeling of abundance, than by writing my conclusion in such a fabulous location. I was inspired after reading '*Rich as F*ck*' by Money Mentor, Amanada Frances, who reflects on her own experience in a similar luxury rooftop pool. Perhaps it was the same one?

The difference is that I know I belong here. This isn't an attempt to 'be in the vibration of my future', I booked this trip without hesitation, when I decided that I wanted this book writing process to be fun. Someone had offered me good luck, when I told them about my intention to write my first book, as the experience was likely to 'be a nightmare'. I reminded myself, right then and there that you get to choose your experiences in life, and I wasn't going to make this process a chore, that needed to be ticked off a list.

As a self-confessed gypsy at heart, travel has always been in my blood, and after a post pandemic world, I was itching to get away and feel free again. Travel for me, is my love language and there is nothing better than the feeling of expansiveness and excitement at the thought of a new adventure.

Even with this intentionality, and full self-permission, and knowing that I was worthy enough to be here, I still had a moment of self-doubt, before pushing 'confirm' on my flight booking.

'Was it frivolous to travel half-way round the world, just to be in the amplified energy of wealth?'

Was it selfish to leave my kids at home, to work?

Because here's the thing, uplevelling your relationship with money, is never going to be a one-and-done process. It's a continual evolution, that will always be a work in progress.

Equally, your path to riches, is unlikely to be a linear journey from rags to riches. As demonstrated within my own journey, sometimes you need to *really* get the lesson before you learn from it and move on.

Sometimes your beliefs are sneaky, and show up in unexpected ways, and therein lies the magic.

You are never going to be finished, you are a masterpiece that is unfolding like a beautiful painting on a canvas, that has more and more brushstrokes added to it.

Your potential is unlimited and there will always be another level of success and abundance available to you, when you follow the steps contained withing this book, to recognise any challenge, as the opportunity for growth that it is.

You are worthy because you are.

You are good enough because you are.

You are an absolute badass, who is here to shine her light, and make the world a better place.

With every new empowered decision and moment around money, you redefine society's expectations, and change the game for the generations to come.

This is your time, to step into greatness, and become a Wealthy Woman, and I'm cheering you on every step of the way.

Love Rebecca xx

About The Author

Rebecca Barr is an Award-Winning Entrepreneur, Business Growth Strategist for visionary female CEOs, and a Wealth Activator for women. She is also a busy Mumma to 5 young children, and evidence, that if she can do it, you do it too.

After years in corporate, as a HR Manager, she evolved into the Badass, she is Today, when through necessity, she accidentally became an entrepreneur. She started by scaling a Barber Shop, tripling its turnover within the first year, then scaled quickly by adding various brick-and-mortar and online businesses to her portfolio.

After finding a love of coaching and mentorship, by mentoring young students at her local college, she grew her business organically to the 6-figure success it is Today.

She is a fierce champion of women in business, referring over 6 figures in client referrals to other female-led businesses, and is an advocate that women supporting women, needs to be more than a hashtag.

She supports her clients and community, with flexible development solutions, that meet them at every point in their journey.

The Wealthy Woman Mastermind & Retreats – Where wealth-building and integrity is always the vibe, this is the table with the higher-level conversations and industry changing female leadership.

The Wealthy Woman Academy – The ultimate wealth activation academy, designed to awaken your inner Wealthy Woman, so that you can fully own your gifts in your purpose driven business, create a life better than your dreams and become a vibrational match to millions.

Manifest Your Bestseller – A 12 month writing program to write, launch and self-publish your future, legacy based, bestselling book.

For more details of each, please visit her website www.thefemalepreneurcoach.co.uk

Free Resources

Visit her You Tube Channel – The Femalepreneur Coach
Listen to her Podcast – The Femalepreneur Coach

Stay Connected!

Instagram

@thefemalepreneurcoach
@thegoodgirlsguideto

Post-Writing Musings

The journey of writing this book has been such a beautiful process, and a real opportunity for growth as I look back on some of my life experiences, with kinder eyes.

Some of the things that happened when I was young, I hadn't thought about in years and it was great to revisit those moments, from a place of even more growth and empowerment.

Finishing this book has been a very satisfying moment of reflection and if you have ever thought about writing a book, I highly recommend it, even if no one ever buys it, just as a moment of reclaiming and reframing your own story.

In true Manifesting Generator style, most of this work came together in a very intentional period at the end, and again I was reminded that even though I don't do things like most other people, I can ALWAYS rely on myself to get the job done.

I am always supported by The Universe, and the right inspiration and words will always come when I need them. I learned once, that rather than this meaning I'm a disorganised hot mess, this character trait of 'pulling it out the bag' in the eleventh hour, is actually a sign of high performance and I'm finally accepting it.

The subjects and journey of the book, that I have covered within these pages, were not the intentions of my original thoughts as to how this book would look. I have learned far more into the energetic and spiritual principals that support me, than the psychological and strategic elements that I first intended.

I think it was needed. I think no one needed another 'sales strategy' book, but everyone needs a moment to remind themselves how powerful, supported, loved, and connected they are.

My intention with this book, is that this can be a new (excuse the pun) chapter of creativity for me, so if you have enjoyed the book, please make sure you pass it on, leave a review and share it with others. I want this to be part of a new movement for female entrepreneurs who are soulfully showing up for their clients, stepping into their most empowered and abundant self, entirely on their own terms. Your participation in sharing this book and embodying its values will be integral part of that process. Thank you x

Claim Your Wealthy Woman Free Resources

CLAIM YOUR
Wealthy Woman

FREE RESOURCES BY
SCANNING THIS QR
CODE

Printed in Great Britain
by Amazon

40387972R00066